Penguin Nature Guides

Birds

of Lake, River, Marsh and Field

Lars Jonsson

Translated from the Swedish by Roger Tanner
Edited and adapted by Jim Flegg

Penguin Books

Penguin Books Ltd, Harmondsworth,
Middlesex, England
Penguin Books, 625 Madison Avenue,
New York, New York 10022, U.S.A.
Penguin Books Australia Ltd, Ringwood,
Victoria, Australia
Penguin Books Canada Ltd, 2801 John Street,
Markham, Ontario, Canada L3R 1B4
Penguin Books (N.Z.) Ltd, 182–190 Wairau Road,
Auckland 10, New Zealand

Fåglar i naturen: Sjö, å, träsk och åkermark
first published by Wahlström & Widstrand 1977
This translation published 1978

Printed in Portugal by Gris Impressores, Cacém
Filmset in Monophoto Times by
Northumberland Press Ltd,
Gateshead, Tyne and Wear

Contents

Preface

This volume of the series, together with the two previous ones, covers most of the European biotopes. Birds of the mountain, tundra, forest and taiga regions of northern Europe, the Mediterranean countries and the Alps, and other central European mountain ranges, are considered in further volumes. Each of these first three books is designed as an independent entity, but all of them cover the same geographical area. Thus, the reader will find that any two used in combination are considerably more useful than only one. For instance, *Birds of Wood, Park and Garden*, in combination with this volume, deals with practically all of the perching birds as well as the land birds to be found in its area. *Birds of Sea and Coast*, together with this volume, surveys the water birds.

Some species are described in more than one book. This is because the main emphasis when describing them is on their plumage and behaviour in the particular biotope. For instance, the green sandpiper is shown in juvenile plumage in the volume on sea birds, because in nine cases out of ten it is in that plumage when observed by the seaside. However, in this volume, it is shown in summer plumage, as it would be in its breeding area.

I am grateful to Stellan Hedgren for his close co-operation in all aspects of this study, and to the other ornithologists who helped to establish some of the facts, especially Håkan Delin and Lars Svensson, whose extraordinary powers of observation provided material on markings and field characteristics.

L.J.

Introduction

This is the third book in a series of five which includes all bird species breeding or regularly found in Europe. Each volume covers one of the five different types of natural environments. This one is mainly concerned with birds living in or by lakes and other fresh waters, in various kinds of wetlands, on moorland and in agricultural areas. The catchment area comprises Europe south of the coniferous region and north of the Mediterranean countries, excluding the Alps, the Carpathians and other high mountain areas in central Europe.

Birds cannot be easily divided according to biotope: they are extremely mobile, migrate long distances and often display different forms of behaviour and food preferences at different times of the year. This is taken into consideration by including some species in more than one volume. Otherwise most of the species which breed in forests, woods or gardens, but which look for some of their food on farmland (pigeons, starling, jackdaw, thrushes and finches), have been excluded. A number of wetland and moorland species mostly found near the Mediterranean and the Black Sea and to some extent in Hungary, but which breed locally further north, have also been excluded or are only mentioned briefly (little egret, great white heron, squacco heron, spoonbill, little bustard, pratincole, whiskered tern, short-toed lark, Cetti's and Dartford warblers). On the other hand, species which breed north of the catchment area but regularly visit or winter in wetlands and lakes further south have been included (except some waders: see p. 70). Species such as golden eagle, rough-legged buzzard, merlin, snowy owl, shore lark, brambling, Lapland bunting and snow bunting, which breed in northern areas but which may also appear further south during the breeding season are not included. Some species which have escaped from waterbird collections or have been introduced to Europe are also omitted: snow goose, mandarin and ruddy ducks.

5

Birds in their environment

A biotope is the more or less restricted niche of the environment in which a particular type of bird exists. Thus, freshwater lakes, directly or indirectly, are the environment of a large number. Depending on their size and the availability of food, shelter and nesting places, different kinds of lake and shore attract a varied bird fauna. There are distinct differences between eutrophic and oligotrophic lakes. The most abundant bird populations are found in eutrophic and, usually, shallow lowland lakes and ponds in clay regions where the shallow water and abundant nutrients produce a richness of sheltering vegetation and food. In a lake of this kind there are vegetation zones spreading from the shoreline outwards. If the surrounding land is low-lying, the 'shore' – defined as the area between the highest and lowest water levels – can include considerable areas of waterlogged meadows, swamps and ditches that are thick with osiers, alder, willow and an abundance of plants such as sedges, yellow flag and purple loosestrife. This zone also supports frogs and many different insect species. Birds such as snipe, Baillon's crake, yellow wagtail, sedge and aquatic warblers, bluethroat, penduline tit and reed bunting all breed there. Storks, harriers, waders, pipits and other groups of birds rest and feed in this zone. Arrowhead, frog-bit, burr-reed and flowering rush often grow in shallow water, providing food for little grebe, coot, moorhen, various ducks and the mute swan, among others. Beyond the shore, where the lake seldom dries out, there are distinct, often very thick, belts of *Phragmites*, reed mace and sedges. This zone provides swimming birds with an indispensable sanctuary for breeding. The marsh harrier, black-headed gull, several ducks and the mute swan nest on islands and banks of dead reeds. An abundant supply of insects, molluscs and other small creatures feeds a large number of bird species. A number of perching birds, such as reed, great reed and Savi's warbler, and the bearded reedling, have become completely adapted to the special *Phragmites* environment. Outside this zone there is a belt of plants with leaves and flowers floating on the surface, but rooted to the bed of the lake or pond by long stalks. Waterlily, pondweeds and amphibious persicaria are good examples. Such plants are a major food source for ducks, mute swans and coots. Further out still, where the water is deeper, there are submerged plants like spiked water milfoil, hornwort and Canadian pondweed. All of these are food for diving ducks and coots. Other diving water birds, which mainly live on fish and other aquatic creatures, more often search for their food in clear water where plants are less common. Still water often encourages duckweeds floating on or

Shoveler (*Spatula clypeata*) male in full plumage   7 below the surface (ivy duckweed) which are valuable for their high protein content.

Freshwater plant communities accommodate a large number of insects, the staple diet of many species in the food-chain. Chironomidae (non-biting midges), often represented by more than a hundred species in a single lake, are devoured at various stages of their development by predatory insects, fish fry, adult fish, spiders, grebes, young duck, crakes and waders. The enormous concentration of swallows and swifts, black- and white-winged black terns and black-headed and little gulls over such a lake is eloquent testimony to the lavish insect population.

Food-chains in fresh water can often be long and complex. The system is a more or less closed one, where everything is consumed and re-used, and where the balance between the various forms of life is very sensitive to change. Light, temperature and the availability of oxygen and nutrients govern the growth of plants, of which the smallest and simplest are plant plankton, which in turn are devoured by insect larvae and fish fry, the smaller grebes and young duck. The food-chain lengthens and branches, involving many plant and animal species, including herons, ospreys, marsh harriers and, at the end of the chain, man himself.

From all points along the food-chain dead matter falls to the bottom of the lake, where its nutrient content is liberated by bacteria and fungi for re-use. The addition of a large quantity of nutrient salts (mostly nitrogenous and phosphorous impurities) to a lake via sewage and ground-water causes an over-production of plant life, and upsets the balance. This is what happens when rainwater leaches nitrates from farmland and forestry plantations that have been treated with artificial fertilizer (especially if they have been over-fertilized), or when phosphates from detergents are discharged into lakes via the sewerage network. The increased output of plant life resulting from this fertilization overloads the degradation process on the lake bed, with the result that the oxygen is consumed, the nutrient salts are released and there is a further steep rise in vegetation. The choking up of a eutrophic lake in lowland surroundings is a natural but slow process, but badly-planned artificial manuring, coupled with changes in ground-water levels, drainage operations and other forms of wetlands exploitation is regrettable from an ecological point of view.

Oligotrophic lakes are normally situated at higher altitudes: they are deep and often located in rocky areas. Their plant output is smaller, and animal plankton is more numerous than plant plankton. Salmon species predominate among the fish population, and the commonest birds tend to be fish-eaters: the black-throated diver, goldeneye and goosander. The common gull is another typical inhabitant of oligotrophic lakes and their surroundings. There is, of course, no hard and fast boundary between different types of lake, and intermediates do occur.

Rivers and flowing water

Flowing waters are 'open' systems in that they have a steady intake and discharge of nutrients and organisms. They also have an abundant flora and insect fauna which have adapted to life in flowing water. Insects, for example, may have hooks or suckers, or may tend to inhabit cavities under stones. The kingfisher, dipper and grey wagtail are three characteristic species found where there is flowing water.

Wetlands

The term 'wetlands' includes bogs, meadows, marshes, fens and other land which is either partly under or adjoins water. Land of this kind was once considered worthless for industry and agriculture. Now, however, despite an awareness of its ecological importance, it is all too often sacrificed to commercial development. In the last few hundred years the increased amount of acreage needed for food cultivation has led to the draining of most of the wetlands in many areas of Europe, while other wetlands have been reclaimed for industrial uses. The benefits to agriculture are often questionable because drainage may lower the water table elsewhere. Hardly any other change in the landscape in recent times has had such devastating effects on the environment of so many plants and animals. The black stork and white stork, Baillon's crake, great snipe, black-tailed godwit, black- and white-winged black tern and aquatic warbler are examples of wetland species whose numbers have sharply declined in northern and western Europe. Wetlands are important sources of food supply and of vital importance to the livelihood of a rich and varied fauna, and they should therefore be preserved and protected. Moreover, local climate and the local water table are also affected by the condition of lakes and wetlands.

Farmland

Most of Europe's farmland has been reclaimed from broadleaved forests and, to some extent, from wetlands. Thus both types of environment are closely intertwined, biologically speaking. This is the reason for the abundant birdlife in agricultural areas. The food and environment provided by the cultivated crops are two ingredients. Copses and hedges, gardens, ponds and ditches between arable fields, and the great variety of plants growing along roadsides, field headlands and in uncultivated areas are the most important features of the cultivated landscape for the majority of birds.

The current trend of agricultural development is towards monocultures, larger acreages of a single crop. To make this kind of farming efficient there must be larger fields, which means clearing trees and hedges, draining wetlands and the extensive use of pesticides and fertilizers. All of these factors are a negative influence on many of the birds. The nutrients and toxic substances spread over farmland are carried by drainage water into lakes, which also affect that environment.

Field identification and the outward structure of birds

Plumage

In order to properly study a bird's appearance, it is necessary to become familiar with its outward characteristics and the ornithological terminology that describes them. Birds differ from other animals in two unique ways: they have plumage and they can fly.

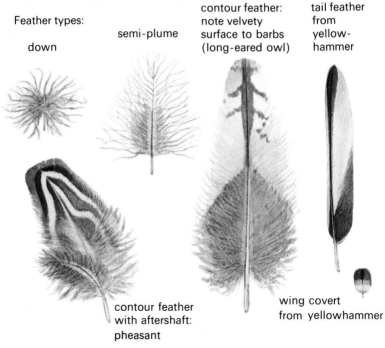

Feather types:

down

semi-plume

contour feather: note velvety surface to barbs (long-eared owl)

tail feather from yellow-hammer

contour feather with aftershaft: pheasant

wing covert from yellowhammer

Birds have two main types of feathers: down and contour. In some orders the chicks emerge from the egg covered in down, which enables them to keep warm. This is a feature of species whose young are left alone in the nest at a very early age (raptors and owls) and also of species whose young leave the nest immediately (ducks and game birds). The outer 'shell' of the adult bird is made up of coverts which cover the underlying insulating down. Many of the coverts attached to the body have a downy lower portion. Some groups, such as game birds, also have an extra feather in the form of down attached to the quill of the covert. The feathers are located in bands or tracts over the body, each tract forming a distinct area of the outward shape. Feather structures and typical markings are illustrated on the facing page.

Moulting

Moulting, the replacement of feathers, is an important stage in the bird's annual cycle. Most species replace their tail and wing feathers once a year. Body feathers, most of the wing coverts and, often, the scapulars and central tail feathers are changed once or twice a year, three times in exceptional cases. Grebes, dabbling duck, many waders, gulls, terns, wagtails, pipits and warblers change their body feathers twice a year. Moulting is often a complicated process; the basic schedule followed by a species also depends on the available food supply, racial identity and migration times, among other things. When and how often moult occurs in a year, and the order in which the different groups of feathers are shed, is a useful aid in recognizing different species. One often sees birds in the process of moulting which are in an intermediate plumage.

Plumage types

A bird's first real plumage (not counting its initial covering of down) is called juvenile or immature. In many families, including most passerines, this is soon partly or entirely replaced. The young of species in which this happens, such as larks, pipits, thrushes and finches, have feathers of a different structure – sparser and downier and less resistant to wear. Additionally, their juvenile colouring is patterned to give good camouflage. The next plumage is usually acquired by the replacement of body feathers and certain coverts, scapulars and the central tail feathers (although game birds, larks and the bearded reedling change all their feathers). Duck, for example, acquire their first winter or breeding plumage at this time (drakes are always at their most resplendent in winter, when they choose their mates). In the case of dabbling duck, small diving duck and the saw-bills, first winter and adult plumages are similar. Youngsters, however,

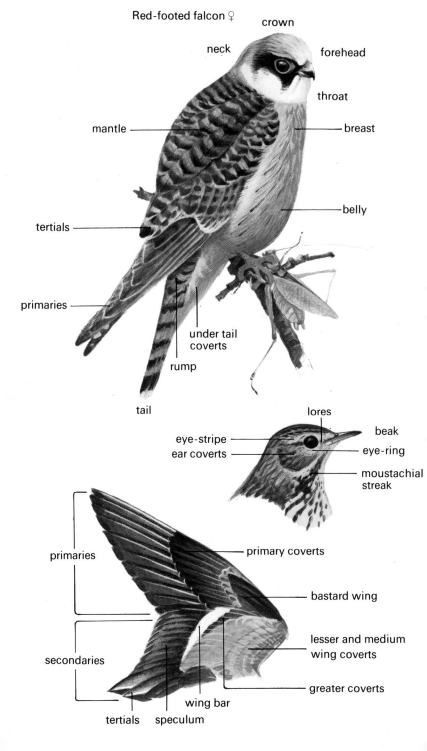

Red-footed falcon ♀

crown

neck

forehead

throat

mantle

breast

belly

tertials

primaries

under tail coverts

rump

tail

lores

beak

eye-stripe

ear coverts

eye-ring

moustachial streak

primaries

primary coverts

bastard wing

secondaries

lesser and medium wing coverts

greater coverts

tertials

speculum

wing bar

acquire their winter plumage later than adults, and sometimes may not reach full plumage until the actual onset of winter.

In many other species, however, full adult plumage is preceded by a varying number of subadult stages. This is a striking feature, for example, among marsh harriers, falcons and gulls. In species which partly or completely change their body feathers twice a year, separate winter and summer plumages can usually be distinguished in the field: grebes, duck, gulls, terns, wagtails and some thrush species. Several passerines 'acquire' summer dress by wearing down the edges of existing feathers. The feathers of the winter or autumn plumage acquired during late summer or autumn have very wide fringes which are worn away, gradually revealing the brighter colours underneath: brambling and reed bunting are two examples. In many species this wear is accompanied by the moulting of certain feathers, as in the wheatear, whinchat and cirl bunting.

Although there may be several plumage stages, three in particular are important:

Juvenile A bird is technically termed juvenile (or immature) until it has begun to acquire its second set of wing feathers. For simplicity, in this book the term applies to a bird with its first set of real feathers. Species which shed their body feathers once or twice before they replace their wing feathers are referred to as juv. autumn, juv. first winter and so on.

Adult – (or mature) is a bird that has developed its full plumage and colouring. If the adult bird has two or more distinguishable plumages during a year, these are termed ad. winter (autumn) and ad. summer (spring). Except where indicated, the illustrations show birds in adult summer or, in the case of duck species, full breeding (winter) plumages.

Subadult A subadult bird is not juvenile but has not yet developed full adult colouring. This is applied to all non-adults.

Appearance and problems of field recognition

There can be a great deal of variation in appearance and plumage within a species. Some species, no matter what their plumage, always have one, or more, conspicuous marking which makes them easily recognizable in most circumstances. Others may have less obvious characteristics and show much individual variation, making it difficult if not impossible to recognize them in the field. Young grebes, duck, harriers, falcons, larks, pipits, warblers and finches are among those which, in certain plumages, tend to defy recognition. Plumage and appearance can vary so widely under different conditions that one must not only learn the basic facts in the

14

A harrier from southern Gotland, May 1976. Its shape, markings and manner of flying reveal that it must be either a pallid or Montagu's harrier. The light grey patches suggest that it is a male, and the predominance of juvenile plumage suggests that it is about one year old. Since the male pallid harrier has a white throat and white breast, the grey, relatively dark throat and breast of this specimen would seem to indicate a Montagu's harrier. The pale collar could belong to a Montagu's harrier of this age.

field manual but also be patient and alert in the field. Note the examples of the enigmatic marsh harrier and skylarks (p. 16).

Calls and song

The identification of calls is an important aspect of field recognition. In fact, it is the most certain way of identifying some species, such as crakes and warblers. The various calls each have a particular function or significance when birds communicate with other members of the same species. These can be functionally classified. In many cases, however, the boundaries between the groups are flexible, and descriptions can only be a rough guide. There is the song or mating call, contact, warning, begging and other calls. Among duck, for instance, where visual signals are more important than vocal ones, the 'song' or, rather, mating call, is usually identical with the contact call.

15

The differentiation between and the significance of the various contact calls are unclear in many respects. Some species, such as the yellow wagtail, have a whole repertoire of contact calls, while in others these calls are used purely to keep the flock together. Sometimes warning and contact calls are combined according to the mood, while in other species they are completely separate and only used appropriately.

Behaviour, habitat and distribution

A bird's behaviour and habitat are of the same importance as appearance and calls as aids to recognition, especially when trying to identify its family or group. A small falcon chasing insects over a fen is probably a red-footed falcon or a hobby. If it sometimes pauses in flight to hover in the air, it is almost certainly a red-footed falcon. (The kestrel also hovers, but it never hunts insects over a fen.) If you flush what seems to be either a short-eared or a long-eared owl, and it perches deep in tree foliage, then it must be the long-eared because the short-eared prefers to sit on the ground, a stone or a fence post. If it sits in a tree it will choose the top, or a branch where it can be clearly seen. On the other hand, be prepared for differences in behaviour from all birds when encountered in unaccustomed surroundings or circumstances.

The distribution and, in the case of migrant birds, the occurrence of the species in relation to the time of year can give some clues to identity. For example, a 'garganey' seen in northern Europe in January is much more likely to be a teal. Individuals of most species, however, and especially migrants, are quite often seen far outside their normal distribution. In this book each description is accompanied by a map of distribution. A key to the use of the maps, and the various signs, is on page 18.

Population density varies a great deal, and it should be remembered that certain species are exceedingly rare or entirely absent in large areas of their overall distribution. We have much more reliable information on distribution in northern, central and western parts of Europe compared with the east and south. As a rule, however, breeding areas tend to be more constant than wintering areas.

Facing page: three skylarks. Top: a fairly worn and unusually pale bird in summer, under overhead sunlight. Centre: a recently moulted and unusually rufous bird in autumn. Bottom: a normal individual sitting in the snow on a dull day and, consequently, well-lit by reflected light from below.

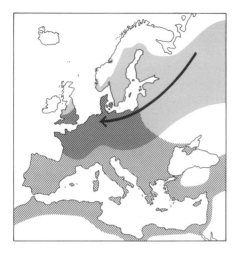

Blue: breeding grounds. Summer visitor only

Blue dots: isolated breeding in colonies

Blue hatched with lines: breeding and over-wintering area

Arrow: main migration route

Grebes *Podicipedidae*

Grebes, specially adapted for living in water, have an ideal anatomy for swimming and diving. Their bodies are cigar-shaped with the legs placed well back. The tail feathers are undeveloped. They nest in various eutrophic fresh waters, very occasionally in sheltered estuaries. They dive for or snap up from the surface of the water their diet of fish, insects, frog spawn and molluscs. Nests are built with pieces of plants in the form of a raft (moored to a water plant) which moves up and down with the water level. During migration and in winter, grebes are often seen on the coast or in larger open waters. Several species are similar to each other in winter and juvenile plumage. For recognition purposes, concentrate on their size (if there are other suitable birds available for comparison), shape, and small but clear differences in the throat, head and bill. The divers, (*Gaviiformes*), which resemble the grebes in many respects, are considerably larger and breed mainly in mountain, moorland and tundra lakes. The black-throated diver (*Gavia arctica*) 58–68 cm, is not uncommon, breeding in large, clear and oligotrophic lakes in Scotland, Scandinavia and northeastern Europe as far south as a line crossing the southern end of the Baltic.

Black-throated diver

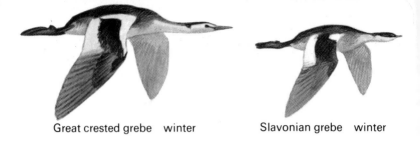

Great crested grebe   winter   Slavonian grebe   winter

Great crested grebe   *Podiceps cristatus*   52 cm

A characteristic bird of many eutrophic lakes – the largest and most easily observed of the grebes. Unmistakable in summer, but can be confused with the red-necked grebe in winter. However, it always has a bright white throat, neck and cheeks, contrasting with the dark narrow crown, which does not extend as far as the eye. Pairs perform striking courtship displays especially early in the breeding season. Often they swim breast-to-breast with ruffs extended, performing snake-like contortions with their heads. Vociferous during the spring, producing a variety of grating, high-pitched notes, including a rolling, heron-like 'aorr' and, during their ceremonies, a repetitive, somewhat rattly 'keck-keck-keck …'. In late summer the young are often betrayed by their persistent, whistling begging call 'vie-vie-vie….'. Great crested grebes breed in reeds or other lake vegetation on large expanses of still, clear water. Most winter off the coast, others on inland waters such as reservoirs. Feed mainly on fish and other small water creatures.

Red-necked grebe   *Podiceps griseigena*   46 cm

Smaller and more compact than the great crested grebe. Easily recognizable in summer plumage, with the striking 'clown' face markings. Winters on coasts, often far out to sea, where it can be distinguished from the great crested grebe by head posture, grey neck and white breast, chin and (to a variable extent) cheek. Also, it has a yellow beak base. Young birds moult into winter plumage in late October. Breeds in eutrophic fresh waters, both large reed-fringed lakes and small ponds. During the breeding season it is shyer than the great crested grebe, but often advertises its presence by its calls – a very loud squealing or water rail-like 'ack' or 'oa-ehk', and cackling and grunting sounds. Lives on fish but, to a greater extent than the great crested grebe, also eats aquatic insect larvae.

Great crested grebe

Red-necked grebe

winter

Great crested grebe

Great crested grebe
juvenile about
2 months

juvenile about 2 months

Red-necked grebe

winter

Little grebe · *Tachybaptus ruficollis* · 25 cm

Noisy but sometimes shy, keeping to the reeds during breeding season. In autumn and winter small flocks accumulate on more open waters. Seldom ventures into the open sea, preferring reservoirs, sheltered estuaries and harbours. The yellowish-brown plumage is a good winter characteristic. It is pictured here in a courtship posture or threat display, when the rear end is fluffed up. Juveniles have a reddish-brown breast and the head is marked with black and white stripes until November–December. Breeds on fresh waters, ranging upwards in size from tiny ponds. Its call is a bubbling or whinnying trill. In breeding season it lives mainly on insects and small molluscs, but also eats fish in winter.

Black-necked grebe · *Podiceps nigricollis* · 30 cm

Can be confused with the Slavonian grebe, but its steep forehead and up-tilted beak make it different from the three larger species. Its drooping 'ear'-tufts have an unkempt look. Best distinguished by its head profile in winter and juvenile plumage. Commonest call is a whining 'iurr-ip'. Breeds on eutrophic lakes, often in small colonies and close to a colony of black-headed gulls which gives some protection from predators. Lives mostly on aquatic insects, sometimes 'straining' them from the water. Often winters on lakes, reservoirs and coastal inlets, occasionally in flocks.

Slavonian grebe · *Podiceps auritus* · 35 cm

In summer its red neck (which can look black from a distance), the brighter fiery orange of the 'ear'-tufts and the head profile distinguish it from the black-necked. Like the red-necked, it winters mainly off the coast, often staying well out to sea. In winter plumage, subtle differences such as the cleaner white of the cheek, flesh-coloured 'reins' and the grey patch above them can be hard to spot, so the profile and overall impression are important criteria. Often breeds in small reed-fringed ponds, but also occurs on larger eutrophic lakes. A noisy bird, both day and night, its commonest note is a rolling, shrill but quite melodious 'hyarr' performed in short series. On its breeding grounds also emits several more prolonged shrieks resembling a water rail. Lives on various small aquatic animals.

Little grebe

Black-necked grebe

Slavonian grebe

22–23

Little grebe

winter

winter

Black-necked grebe

juvenile
autumn

Slavonian grebe
winter

Heron

Purple heron

Heron   *Ardea cinerea*   100 cm

The commonest and most widely distributed heron species in Europe, it can be confused with the slightly smaller purple heron (see below). The crane (see p. 68) has a completely different flight silhouette. Has a majestic look about it, flying heavily on broad, dark and deeply-curved wings. Easily overlooked when resting, stock-still, in a reed-bed. The call is usually a hollow, grating 'kraurnk', but in the breeding grounds it emits a variety of discordant sounds and beak-clatterings. Occurs in widely varied habitats, feeding near water, and breeding nearby in bulky nests of twigs and branches, usually built in trees. Other colonies occur in reed-beds and sometimes, on the Atlantic coast, on cliffs. Lives on fish, small animals and insects.

Purple heron   *Ardea purpurea*   80 cm

Looks darker than the heron, with a slender snake-like head and neck. Can be mistaken in flight for a heron, but has a more angular throat and detectably longer hind claws. Young birds take several years to develop full colouring. In flight the wing coverts are a dull shade of reddish fawn to mauvish brown. Seen less often in the open than the heron and must be flushed from dense marshland vegetation. Sometimes emits a heron-like (though less tinny) note when taking to the wing, but otherwise is silent. Breeds in colonies in reed-beds. Same diet as the heron.

Heron

Purple heron

Heron

juvenile

juvenile

Purple heron

Bittern

Little bittern *Ixobrychus minutus* 35 cm

Rare in western Europe, commoner elsewhere. Retiring but less elusive than the bittern. Usually runs away when in danger, or adopts an upright camouflage position. When flushed, often flies only a short distance, sometimes climbing part-way up in the reeds and eyeing the intruder. The male is unmistakable in flight, and the female has the same, but less distinct, pattern. The unusual flight of fast jerky wing beats alternates with glides and abrupt twists and turns. Most active at dusk, when its call is often drowned by the frogs' chorus. Mating call is a low, grunting 'grok' repeated at two-second intervals. Frequents dense shore zone vegetation beside lakes, wide rivers and other wetland areas.

Bittern *Botaurus stellaris* 76 cm

Lives such a retiring life in dense *Phragmites* beds that it is often only noticed because of its distinctive sound. The male's short foghorn-like blasts are mainly heard in spring and often at night. Repeated at intervals of about two seconds, they may be audible for five km. Resembles a cross between a heron and an owl. When flying low above the reeds the neck is often half stretched out, but when flying over long distances, its neck is contracted. Adopts an upright camouflage posture when approached. Lives on fish, frogs and other small creatures, including waterbird eggs and chicks.

Little bittern

Bittern

Little bitter

juvenile

♂

♀

Bittern

White stork *Ciconia ciconia* 102 cm

Easily recognized and still familiar, even though its numbers have diminished considerably since the end of the nineteenth century. Has disappeared altogether from parts of western and northern Europe. Climatic changes, the draining of fens and the use of pesticides are the main causes of the decline. The white stork is still common, however, in open farming country in eastern Europe, feeding on all kinds of small creatures such as frogs, snakes, fish, rodents, worms and nestlings. Often seen sedately strutting along in short grass. Breeds in large twiggy nests built in trees and in natural or man-made sites, on buildings and telegraph poles. A loud beak-rattling greets the returning bird at the nest. During the migration to Africa enormous numbers of white storks converge on Gibraltar and the Bosphorus to take advantage of the shortest sea crossings.

Black stork *Ciconia nigra* 97 cm

Like the white stork, easily recognizable. Note, however, that in back-lighting and from a distance, the white stork seems dark: the white of its upper parts can be confused with the sunlight's glitter on the black stork. Breeds in unspoiled old woodlands but feeds in fens and wet meadows in eastern Europe, often side by side with the white stork. Produces a soft whining and a beak clatter in and near the nest. Its numbers have also declined, and large collections are only seen when migrating, in families, usually about a month later than the white stork. Same diet as the white stork.

White stork

Black stork

White stork

Black stork

White stork

Geese, swans and ducks   *Anatidae*

All geese, swans and ducks, adapted to swimming and finding their food on or in the water, have webbed feet, buoyant bodies with dense, highly waterproof plumage over a thick layer of down, and long necks. Wing feathers are shed so quickly, at the end of summer, that the birds are grounded for only a short time. The down-covered young can swim within a few moments after hatching and are then able to feed themselves. Geese, swans and ducks are customarily divided into the following subfamilies:

Swans (subfamily *Cygninae*).

Geese (subfamily *Anserinae*). See p. 34.

Dabbling ducks (subfamily *Anatinae*) are found mainly in shallow eutrophic lakes and brackish water, but are common along sea coasts in winter. They graze on water plants by up-ending their bodies in shallow water, can sift small creatures and seeds out of the surface water (see teal, p. 41) or mud, and take-off almost vertically from the water's surface. Ducks, young, and drakes in eclipse often look very similar. Speculum colour, shape and size, markings, head and bill colour and calls are often important recognition criteria. When dabbling ducks are seen from a distance sitting on the water, the speculum may be concealed. Then the observer must know shape, posture and plumage pattern differences between species. Their diet is plants and small creatures.

Diving ducks (*Aythyinae*) dive for their food. Their take-off begins with a pattering across the water and a beating of wings in order to accelerate. Most diving ducks breed in fresh water but often winter by the sea. Distinguished from dabbling ducks by triangular head profiles and dumpy bodies. Two other species commonly breed in Europe. The scaup (*Aythya marila*), which lives beside mountain lakes and along the Baltic coasts, resembles the tufted duck with which it is often seen during winter along sea coasts and on fresh waters nearby. The scaup drake has a mottled grey back and no tuft and the duck has a large white patch around the bill base. Barrow's goldeneye (*Bucephala islandica*) lives in Iceland. Diving ducks often have similar wing markings, so shape and colouring differences are the most important recognition criteria. Water creatures are important in the diet of the goldeneye, scaup and tufted duck, while the other species live mainly on water plants.

The sawbills. The smew, red-breasted merganser and goosander (*Merginae*) form a subgroup of the diving ducks. Their long, narrow, serrated bills make them adept at catching fish. They rise from the water like diving ducks. Of the three species, the red-breasted merganser (*Mergus serrator*) mainly frequents mountain lakes, rivers and occasionally sea coasts, but it can also be seen on large expanses of clear fresh water. It is similar to the goosander, but the drake has a reddish-brown breast, dark mottled flanks and a more splayed-out crest. The duck goosander has a smoother colour transition between head and neck and a less splayed-out crest than the duck merganser.

Early autumn. Top: wigeon in eclipse. Middle: two mallard ducks and a moulting drake. Bottom: teal and a young garganey (extreme right).

Whooper swan   *Cygnus cygnus*   152 cm

Distinguished from the mute swan by its predominantly yellow waxy beak, straighter neck posture and its call. The young are greyer and more evenly marked than those of the mute swan, and the pale pink beak stands out light against the dark head. The opposite applies to the mute swan. The note is a loud, often varied and melodious trumpeting. In flight it produces shorter honkings. Bewick's swan (*Cygnus bewickii*) is noticeably smaller and has less yellow on its bill. It breeds in the Siberian tundra, winters on marshes by the sea in western Europe but only rarely visits inland lakes. The whooper swan breeds beside lakes in marshland and tundra and winters beside lakes and on the coast. It migrates in flocks and often becomes a brief but regular annual visitor at suitable lakes along its route. It lives on water plants and also on grass, on which it grazes in coastal meadows.

Mute swan   *Cygnus olor*   152 cm

One of our best-known birds. The young are distinguished from those of the whooper swan by their beak marking and browner colour. Most young birds moult during autumn and become very motley-looking. They are then easy to recognize even at a distance, because the whooper swan young are always a uniform shade of grey until about December. In flight the wings make a swishing sound which is not heard from whooper or Bewick's swans. The mute swan is often tame and occurs in many parks. It prefers to breed on eutrophic fresh waters. It migrates irregularly in northern and eastern Europe. Lives on vegetation pulled from the lake bed, and will graze grasses and cereal crops.

Whooper swan

Mute swan

juvenile

Whooper swan

Mute swan

juvenile

Canada goose *Branta canadensis* 92–102 cm

Introduced to the British Isles and Sweden from Canada, this bird has become wild and can be very bold. It breeds primarily on large lakes, often in parkland. Its call is a loud braying 'aa-hoa', with the second syllable rising in pitch.

Greylag goose *Anser anser* 76–89 cm

The only goose species breeding in the area (see above) outside the mountain and forest regions of northern Europe. Its strikingly pale grey wing coverts and stout pinkish-orange beak and feet make it different in appearance from other geese. Greylags in southeastern Europe are pale with pinker bills than the western type. The call is similar to the domestic goose. Breeding grounds are bogs, reeds bordering lakes and coastal islands. Lives mostly on vegetable food, often grazes in meadows and fields, and will attack potato crops.

The goose species which breed in northern and Arctic areas and winter in Europe can all be seen on ploughed fields, stubbles, pastures and beside fresh water inland. Bean goose, pink-footed goose and white-fronted goose can all be found feeding or roosting a long way inland.

Bean goose *Anser fabalis* 71–89 cm

Distinguished from the greylag by its bill and feet colour, darker neck and head and much duller wing marking in flight. The pink-footed goose (*A. brachyrhynchus*) 61–71 cm has the pale grey upper parts of the greylag with the flanks the darkest portion of its body. It has pink feet and bill, and is squatter, with a short neck and a dark head with blunter profile. Noisier than the bean goose, its calls have a lighter timbre. The white-fronted goose (*Anser albifrons*) 66–76 cm has a white patch at the beak base and irregular black bars across the belly (although not in young birds). Has a higher-pitched call than the bean goose, a somewhat vibrant 'kay-ly'. The note of the bean goose, a variable bi- or trisyllabic 'kayak' or 'kaya-kak', is more tuneful than the greylag's honking. Geese often spend the winter in large flocks and fly in V-formation.

Canada goose

Greylag goose

Bean goose

juvenile

White-fronted goose

Canada goose

Greylag goose

Bean goose

Pink-footed goose

Mallard ♀   Gadwall ♀

Mallard *Anas platyrhynchos*   51–62 cm

The most numerous and widespread of the dabbling ducks. The drake in breeding plumage is unmistakable, and in eclipse is distinguished from the female by a uniformly greenish-yellow beak. The duck's colour and marking vary considerably, but in eclipse she looks generally darker. Her orange beak has dark markings on the upper mandible. The duck's call is a loud croaking – its tone and syllabic composition vary according to mood, but it is harsh and penetrating when disturbed. The drake's call is a subdued, nasal, rather frog-like 'vairp'. During courtship in late autumn he makes a low whistling 'pyu'. The mallard breeds beside most kinds of fresh water and often appears, without any vestige of shyness, on park lakes where food is offered. It can also be seen in large flocks on estuaries and coasts in winter. The varied diet includes plant and animal matter.

Gadwall *Anas strepera*   51–56 cm

Slightly smaller and slimmer than the mallard. In all plumages it can be recognized by its black and white speculum (but cf. wigeon). On the water the black under-tail of the drake in breeding plumage is a recognition characteristic, while birds in other plumages can be recognized by beak colour with a yellow-orange bar along the lower edge. The wigeon-like white belly is a typical feature in flight. The often-noisy duck's call is louder and shriller than the mallard. Near the nest it utters a mechanically repetitive warning note, 'ehk'. The drake's lower, hoarser 'errp', is similar to the garganey's. Can be found on fresh and brackish waters with plenty of vegetation along the shoreline. Outside the breeding season it can also be seen on small ponds and flooded marshes. Its diet is as varied as the mallard's.

Mallard

Gadwall

♂ eclipse

♂

Mallard

♀

juvenile

Gadwall

♀

♂

Pintail ♀

Shoveler ♀

Pintail *Anas acuta*

♂ 61–76 cm ♀ 51–57 cm

The drake is unmistakable, and the duck, too, is often recognizable by her long neck and tail. The round head shapes, even markings and leaden-grey bills are characteristic. Young often have distinctive cinnamon heads. In flight the most striking features are the slender body and wide pale speculum border. A quiet bird, but the drake sometimes emits a teal-like 'krily', while the duck has a low-pitched croak. Usually breed in small numbers on rough grazing marshland where vegetation is sparse, occasionally beside lowland lakes with thick reed banks. They winter mostly on the coast, often with other dabbling ducks. The diet leans more towards vegetable matter than the mallard's. Pintails sometimes join mallards in stubble fields, looking for waste corn.

Shoveler *Anas clypeata*

51 cm

An unusual bill shape makes a distinctive profile, both in the forward-tilted posture on the water and in rapid flight. The blue-grey (♂) to greenish-grey (♀ juvenile) wing coverts are usually very noticeable in flight. During spring evenings this shy bird can often be seen in pairs or small groups making courtship flights at great speed with sudden twists and turns over the lake where they nest. The drake emits a double staccato 'vack-ack' and the duck a more mallard-like prolonged 'veck-eck'. Found near eutrophic lowland lakes and marshes, shovelers live mainly on small aquatic animals and seeds, filtered from mud and water with the comb-like beak edges. Two or three birds will often feed close together, stirring up nourishing particles from the bottom of shallow waters.

Pintail

Shoveler

juvenile

♀

Pintail

♂

♂ eclipse

♀

Shoveler ♂

♀ Teal   ♀   ♀

Garganey

Teal   *Anas crecca*   35–39 cm

Our smallest duck, which may be confused only with the garganey. Even in breeding plumage the drake can appear nondescript unless it is clearly seen. However, most are characterized by pale markings on the sides of the rump and inside the base of the tail (cf. the garganey and p. 31). In flight the two white bars on the speculum are a typical feature, although in the drake the innermost of the two is more like an oblong patch. A conspicuously buoyant, often nervous and jerky bird which, like a phalarope, springs from the water with the greatest of ease. The drake has a short, bell-like 'krrip' or 'krick', while the duck quacks shrilly and takes off with a soft, rolling 'trrr'. Teal usually occur in flocks (even when breeding) on lowland lakes and in lagoons and brackish water behind the sea coast. Some breed in lowland marshy areas, others beside small mountain lakes. Seeds are a large portion of their diet, which also includes other vegetable matter and small creatures.

Garganey   *Anas querquedula*   40 cm

May be confused with the teal, but sits lower in the water, tilted further forward and its tail and wings poke up at an angle. The head is more oblong, the beak stouter and the head (in ducks with full colouring) more distinctly barred. In flight the drake's wings are distinctively pale blue-grey, darker in the case of the duck and young birds, but always paler than the teal's. The drake's croaking rattle is unmistakable. The duck has teal-like quacks. A shy elusive bird, not often found outside its African wintering areas, the garganey prefers eutrophic lakes surrounded by waterlogged marshes. Migrants may pause beside quite small waters in open country. Arrives late in spring and departs during August and September. Lives on seeds, plant material and small animals.

Teal

Garganey

40–41

Teal

juvenile

♂

♀

♀

Garganey

♂

♂ eclipse

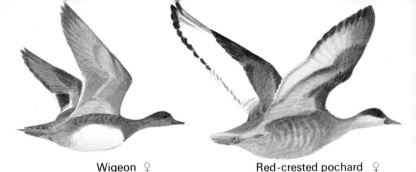

Wigeon ♀   Red-crested pochard ♀

Wigeon *Anas penelope* 44–50 cm

The shape is more like a diving duck than other dabbling ducks. In breeding season it is commonest beside northern forest lakes bordered by bogs and grassy swamps but is most often seen along the coast during spring migration. From mid-August large flocks rest on eutrophic lowland lakes, packed closely together like coots to stock up with food from the plants on the water's surface. Colours in these autumnal flocks vary considerably from the dull brownish grey of young ducks to the deep wine-red eclipse dress of older drakes. Adult drakes in flight are distinguished by dazzling white wing patches. Has a typical flight silhouette, with white belly, short pointed tail, long wings and 'knobbly' head. Drakes whistle a melodious 'hui-oo' and ducks have a grating 'oarr, oarr, oarr...'. Mainly a plant feeder, with its short blunt beak ideal for cropping marsh grasses. Feeds on seaweed in muddy estuaries and bays in winter.

Red-crested pochard *Netta rufina* 55–59 cm

Mallard-sized. Two striking features of the drake are a red bill and crown feathers which fluff up when he is roused. In eclipse the drake closely resembles the duck, an even greyish brown with pale grey cheeks, but has the scraggy remnants of his fox-red crest plus his red bill. Looks very large in flight, with broad, dazzling white wing bars. Its commonest call is a short, mechanical and hasty barking 'err'. The drake, during courtship, emits a note something like 'at-choo'. During typical courtship flight over the breeding grounds, several drakes will pursue a duck at great height. Found locally and irregularly in Europe in shallow coves cut off from the sea, on salt pans, lowland lakes and eutrophic river deltas. At one time it was found on the salt steppe lakes in central Asia. Although classed as a diving duck, its eating habits are more like dabbling ducks because it up-ends and filters.

Wigeon

Red-crested pochard

♂

♀

Wigeon

♂ eclipse

♀

Red-crested pochard ♂

Pochard ♀   Tufted duck ♀   Ferruginous duck ♀

Pochard   *Aythya ferina*   44–47 cm

The drake is unmistakable. The duck is nondescript, but her head and bill shape is highly characteristic. Both are distinguished in flight from other diving ducks by grey, not white, wing bars. The duck's call is a grating 'krra, krra, krra...', while during courtship the drake emits a low whistling 'pue, pue, pue...'. Breeds beside eutrophic lakes with large expanses of open water. Drakes heavily outnumber ducks. Feeds on seeds, plants and small water creatures.

Tufted duck   *Aythya fuligula*   41–46 cm

The only duck species with a tuft on its head. Females vary in appearance and are occasionally white under the tail (cf. ferruginous duck) and/or have a white ring around the bill base (cf. scaup p. 30). The head is 'round square', with a thick bill shaped like a spoon handle. The duck's call is a grating 'err, err, err...', the drake's a gently vibrating whispering whistle. Breeds beside lakes with large expanses of clear water. In winter there are often large flocks in lowland lakes, reservoirs and in brackish water near the sea. Feeds on small creatures, seeds and plants, although animal food is its mainstay.

Ferruginous duck   *Aythya nyroca*   36–42 cm

Smaller than the tufted duck, but has a bigger head, sloping forehead and longer beak. The white on the belly and under the tail are conspicuous in flight (although these are greyish fawn in young birds and during eclipse). Striking white bar on the wings. During spring the duck is very noisy in flight, emitting an 'err, err, err...' which is similar to but higher pitched than the tufted duck. The drake has a low hissing note. Fairly common in eastern Europe by lowland lakes with dense shoreline vegetation. Unobtrusive, and seldom seen on open water, unlike other diving ducks.

Pochard

Tufted duck

Ferruginous duck

Pochard

♂

♀

♂

Tufted duck

♀

♀

juvenile

Ferruginous duck

♂

Goldeneye
juvenile

♀ ♂ November

Smew

Goldeneye *Bucephala clangula* 40–49 cm

The drake looks very pale from a distance. In breeding plumage the duck is grey with a 'fluffy' reddish-brown head which looks pressed tightly onto the white neck. The young are nondescript greyish brown with all-dark bills and dark eyes. The drakes' wing beats produce a characteristic whistling noise. During courtship he emits a noisy quick-fire 've-veyeck' followed by a garganey-like creaking sound. The duck has a rapid, grating 'berr, berr, berr'. Breeding may be in nestboxes and holes deserted by other birds near clear forest lakes and ponds, often close to rivers and waterfalls. Outside the breeding season individuals or small flocks visit lakes, reservoirs, rivers and the coast. Feeds on molluscs, insect larvae and some seeds.

Smew *Mergus albellus* 41 cm

With a breeding biology similar to the goldeneye, the two species sometimes produce hybrids. A winter visitor, either singly or in small flocks, on open lakes, reservoirs and coastal inlets. The duck's most conspicuous feature is her white cheek. The drake does not acquire his unmistakable and magnificent breeding plumage until November. In flight the smew is a true sawbill, slender and with elongated neck and rapid wing beats. In flight at a distance, the drake might be confused with a black guillemot in winter dress. Feeds mainly on fish.

Goosander *Mergus merganser* 58–72 cm

Our largest freshwater duck, but may be confused with the red-breasted merganser (see p. 30). In late autumn and winter both sexes have beautiful, peach-coloured underparts which fade in spring. The drake in eclipse and young birds resemble the duck, although their crests are less conspicuous. The duck emits a loud rolling 'skrrak, skrrak, skrrak...'. The drake's spring call is a beautiful ringing double note. Nests in hollow trees near lakes and fast-flowing rivers, and occasionally on the coast. In winter it prefers lakes and reservoirs, and occasionally the coast.

Goldeneye

Smew

Goosander

Goldeneye

♀

♂

Smew

♂

♀

♀

Goosander

♀

♂

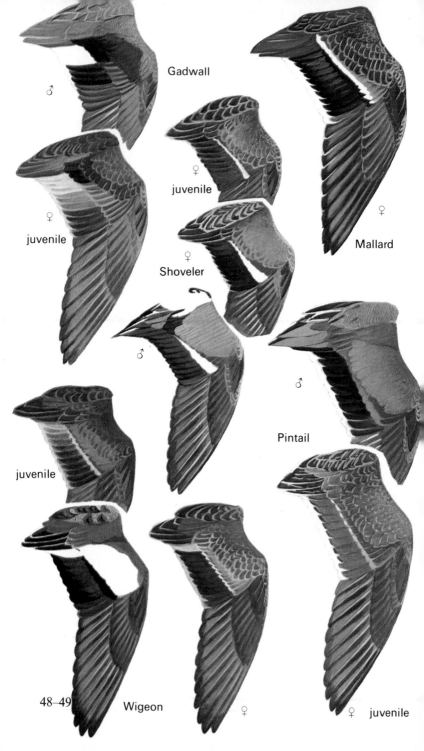

Gadwall

♂

♀
juvenile

♀
juvenile

Mallard

♀

♀
juvenile

Shoveler

♀

♂

♂

Pintail

juvenile

48–49   Wigeon

♀

♀   juvenile

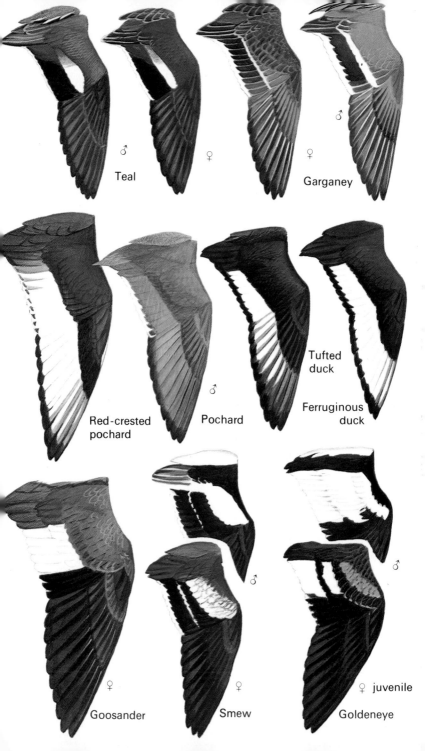

♂

♀

♀

Teal

♂

Garganey

Red-crested
pochard

♂

Pochard

Tufted
duck

Ferruginous
duck

♀

Goosander

♂

♀

Smew

♀ juvenile

♂

Goldeneye

Birds of prey *Falconiformes*

Birds of prey capture and devour living prey – hence their expert flying ability, strong feet, sharp talons and hooked beaks. They are divided into two sub-orders, *Accipitres* (osprey and hawk species) and *Falcones* (falcons). Their habitats when breeding, hunting or migrating reflect their flight capability and special food requirements. The most characteristic species encountered near lakes, marshes and wetlands are the osprey, black kite, harriers and insect-hunting red-footed falcons and hobbies. The black kite, the three harriers, red-footed falcon, hobby and kestrel, however, are found in drier areas, moorland and farmland. Many other species breeding in northern forests also visit these areas. The buzzard (*Buteo buteo*) 62–74 cm often frequents farming country interspersed with woodland or small clumps of trees. Silhouette and behaviour of birds of prey are important recognition features. Harriers, for example, hold their wings in a V-shape and falcons have pointed wing tips.

Buzzard

Osprey

juvenile

♂

Osprey   *Pandion haliaetus*   55–69 cm, wing span 145–160 cm

The female and young have a broader brown collar than the male. Behaviour is
distinctive, quite different from other raptors. With shallow slow wing beats it glides
over water with wings at an angle and circles once or twice like a big gull: it climbs,
hovers for awhile, and then resumes its glide. If, when hovering, a fish is sighted
it descends by stages before plunging, often disappearing completely below the water.
The nest is a large accumulation of branches atop a tall pine tree, often some distance
from the nearest water. Its contact call is a loud 'pyipp', but at the nest there is
a repetitive 'pyu, pyu, pyu…' and long whining sounds. Most birds winter in
tropical western Africa and around the western Mediterranean. Their diet is fish.

Black kite   *Milvus migrans*   56–62 cm, wing span 120–145 cm

A large, dark, well-proportioned bird, distinguished from the female marsh harrier by its stockier build, slightly forked tail (not very noticeable in juveniles), the wings held flat or slightly inclined, and the diagonal bar formed across the wing by pale wing coverts. Patiently and slowly it patrols river banks and marshes, usually sliding flat-winged and steering with its tail, reluctantly breaking this routine with occasional deep, slow wing beats to maintain height. It screeches like a young gull, or makes a buzzard-like mewing. It is numerous and gregarious in places, but never breeds in great numbers outside the Mediterranean countries. Nests of twigs are built in densely wooded areas, but it can at times be seen in just about any habitat, including refuse tips. An omnivorous bird, its diet ranges from insects caught on the wing to carrion, refuse, small birds and other animals.

Marsh harrier   *Circus aeruginosus*   48–55 cm wing span 110–125 cm

Easily recognizable as a harrier by its long wings, held in a shallow V, and from its flight, which is sometimes as light as a paper dart and at other times quite floppy. Distinguished from other harriers by its larger size and colour. The chocolate-brown young have red ochre head markings. At least three years elapse before the male acquires the paler areas of plumage, but he breeds at the age of two, despite a drabber plumage. Marsh harriers often fly low above reed-beds, 'quartering' their hunting area and occasionally dropping out of sight as they pounce on prey. The male's courtship flight, at great height, is accompanied by plover-like 'kve-a' notes. The marsh harrier is mainly a bird of large *Phragmites* beds but may hunt over nearby fens and meadows. It is common in suitable habitats, both while breeding and during migration. It lives on all manner of small creatures and birds.

Black kite

Marsh harrier

Juvenile marsh harriers

juvenile

Black kite

♀

Marsh harrier

♂

Hen harrier *Circus cyaneus* 43–50 cm, wing span 100–120 cm

Heavier built than the pallid and Montagu's harrier, but has a similar buoyancy in flight and holds its wings in a V. The male's darker grey head and breast are striking in flight. Young birds are very similar to adult females but have a more distinct pale ruff. Females fly more heavily and have blunter wings than the pallid and Montagu's harrier females. The rump is usually a clearer white than in the other two species. The hen harrier often glides in a slow low wobble across its hunting grounds, tumbling onto its prey in sudden twists and turns. When not hunting it flies much faster. Hunts across bog, moorland, grazing country, reed-beds and coastal meadows. During his courtship flight the male emits a dry chattering 'chuck-uck-uck-uck-uck'. The female's warning call is a piercing 'check-eck-eck-eck...' similar to the great spotted woodpecker's. The hen harrier lives mainly on rodents and young birds.

Montagu's harrier *Circus pygargus* ♂ 40–45 cm ♀ 44–51 cm wing span 100–120 cm

The male is darker grey than the hen and pallid harriers. The bouncy flight is like a tern's, and the birds look very lean and lanky, especially the male. Young birds and females look very much like pallid harriers in corresponding plumage. Differences in head markings are probably the best recognition criteria at close quarters – notice especially the pallid harrier's pale ruff and dark striations across and behind the eye. Year-old males, however, can show a pale ruff formed of unmoulted juvenile feathers. The male's mating call is a shrill 'nyack-nyeck-nyeck', and his contact call a snappy 'knyeck'. The female's begging note is a light whistling 'pih-i', and her warning call a fast, shrill neighing 'check-eck-eck-eck...'. Found on moorland, meadows and marshlands, it lives on small animals and birds such as larks and pipits, rodents and reptiles.

Pallid harrier *Circus macrourus* 38–46 cm, wing span 90–110 cm

A rare visitor from eastern Europe. The male is smaller, more compact and far lighter – almost gull-like – compared with Montagu's harrier. The female and young birds are very similar to Montagu's harrier but have a distinct pale ruff, a dark eyebrow and in rare cases can be conspicuously pale above or behind the eye (see also Montagu's harrier and illustration). Occurs on moorland, cultivated steppe and dry fenland. Its diet includes more insects than Montagu's harrier.

Hen harrier

Montagu's harrier

Pallid harrier

Hen harrier ♂

from beneath

Montagu's harrier ♂

Montagu's harrier

Pallid harrier ♂

Pallid harrier

Hen harrier ♀

Hen harrier ♀

Pallid harrier
juvenile

Montagu's harrier ♀

Montagu's harrier ♀

Pallid harrier ♀

Montagu's harrier

Montagu's harrier ♀   first year ♂

56–57

Red-footed falcon

♀

Red-footed
falcon

♂

Kestrel

♀

♂

juvenile
Hobby

Red-footed falcon *Falco vespertinus*

28–33 cm
wing span 60–65 cm

Small and less compact than the hobby, more like a short-tailed kestrel. The male's coloration is unmistakable. Younger males have dark primaries and one-year-olds have striped underparts. The underparts and crown of the female (see p. 57) range from light sandy yellow, near-white (mainly younger birds) to orange, with varied streaking and grey upper parts. Young birds and females nearly always have a black mask around the eye, never found in the kestrel. A red-footed falcon often perches on telephone wires watching for insects, its short tail instantly distinguishing its silhouette from the kestrel's. It frequently hovers, and at dusk will catch insects on the wing, like the hobby. A gregarious bird, it breeds mostly in colonies, occupying old rooks' nests in clumps of trees on open moorland, cultivated plains or close to wetlands. Frogs and insects are its main diet. Rare in western Europe except on migration in spring or autumn.

Kestrel *Falco tinnunculus*

33–39 cm, wing span 68–80 cm

Easily distinguished from other falcons (except for the south European lesser kestrel) by its long tail, and the flight silhouette which resembles the cuckoo. The female and young are similar, but the bars on her upper parts are less distinct. Frequently hovers, an excellent field characteristic. Often perches on telegraph poles or other conspicuous vantage points. The most widespread falcon, it is common in open country in some places. It breeds solitarily in old nests, on buildings or cliff ledges. A vociferous bird on the nesting grounds, uttering a piercing but somewhat rasping 'ki', sometimes in quick series but sometimes singly. Lives on rodents, birds, frogs and insects.

Hobby *Falco subbuteo*

28–35 cm, wing span 70–80 cm

More compact than the kestrel and red-footed falcon, its pattern of movement is faster and more regular. Long pointed wings and a short tail distinguish its silhouette in flight. Adult birds have red 'trousers' (see p. 57). Young birds differ from the young of the red-footed falcon in their dark crown. The hobby almost invariably captures its prey, mainly larks, swallows and insects, in the air. On summer evenings it often pursues dragon-flies across fens and lakes, flying slowly, more like a red-footed falcon. Breeds in old crows' nests in copses or thinly wooded country. Calls vary: sometimes it is a 'kyue-kyue-kyue...' or 'ki-ki-ki...' similar to the lesser spotted woodpecker. Winters in Africa south of the equator, outside the rain forest region. Migrates in August and September and does not return until May.

Red-footed falcon

Kestrel

Hobby

Red-footed falcon
juvenile

Red-footed
falcon

♂

juvenile

Kestrel

Kestrel

♂

Hobby

Red-legged partridge *Alectoris rufa* 35 cm

Similar to a partridge in flight, but the distinctive orange ochre under the rump frequently protrudes from the otherwise partridge-like tail. The young are even more like partridges before they moult in the autumn, but they show traces of the bib frame and flank markings of the adults (unlike young partridges, which have light striations on flanks and underparts). The courtship call, like the partridge's, is a mechanically and rapidly reiterated sequence of a hoarse 'kotcherr-cherr, kotcherr-cherr . . .'. The alarm call is a hard 'kuck, kuck'. Rather restless in its feeding habits, it moves around more than the partridge, and when in danger is more likely to run than fly. Occasionally it perches on a post or wall. Its favourite haunts are dry, stony or ploughed fields, where it lives on seeds and insects.

Partridge *Perdix perdix* 32 cm

Its shape, bright chestnut head and short rust-coloured tail are conspicuous when taking to the wing. The hen has less distinct belly markings. The fawn-grey young have distinct pale striations. Common in open farming country, living for most of the year in close-knit groups, usually families. Partridges patiently work along tilled ground, roadsides, rows of bushes and other 'edge' areas to find seeds such as knotgrass and catchfly or insects for the young. When startled they take to the wing, one after another, with a loud clatter of wings and a piercing 'pitt, pitt . . . pick . . . prr, pick . . .'. They enjoy sunbathing and rolling in dusty gravel but will run to safety when apprehensive. The courtship call is an explosive metallic 'kierr-ik, kierr-ik . . .' which can be repeated all day. They feed mainly on seeds in summer and autumn, but prefer green plants in winter and spring.

Red grouse *Lagopus lagopus scoticus* 40 cm

A subspecies of willow grouse confined to Britain and Ireland. It looks very dark in flight and on the ground. The hen is a little paler than the cock, and both sexes are fawn, rather than russet, during summer. When taking to the wing its note is a laughing, nasal, almost frog-like 'veugh vehehuhuhuhu', while the courtship call is a steadily accelerating succession of 'go-back go-back rrr . . .'. Common on open moorlands and bogs, its diet is seeds, berries and plant shoots, especially heather, and insects.

Red-legged partridge

Partridge

Red grouse

Red-legged
partridge

♂

♀

Partridge

Red grouse

♂

♀

Pheasant   *Phasianus colchicus*   ♀ 55–62 ♂ 75–90 cm

Imported to Europe from Asia. The colour of the cock varies, depending on race. The pheasant differs from other game birds in size and tail shape. Most often found in small groups in farming country interspersed with woodland, copses, hedges and often in reeds near lakes. The cock's courtship call is a harsh bisyllabic scolding followed by fast noisy wing flutterings. The wings are also very noisy in flight, which, with the metallically hard and hoarse scolding 'ech' flight note, often gives the bird away. Pheasants like a varied diet. Adults live on vegetable food – seeds, fruit, nuts, roots and plants – but the chicks like insects and other small creatures. They often visit places where food is put out for them.

Quail   *Coturnix coturnix*   18 cm

Seldom seen on the breeding grounds but its presence is often revealed in May or June by the courtship call of the cock, a rapidly and rhythmically repetitive trisyllabic whistle on a falling scale, 'quit-quit-it'. Dusk is the best time to hear this 'machine' coming from the clover, potatoes, cornfields and meadows. The hen makes a low 'brit-bit', sometimes synchronized with the final syllable of the cock's call. The quail skims over vegetation with fast, shallow wing beats but soon lands again. It is very difficult to flush, however, and prefers to creep away or lie doggo. Most migrate considerable distances to Africa south of the Sahara, flying in flocks by night. During migration, and especially in southern Europe, it can be found in large numbers in unusual habitats. Numbers visiting northern and western Europe vary greatly from year to year.

Corncrake   *Crex crex*   26 cm

Its closest relatives are the reed-bed crakes, but the corncrake's habitat is lush pasture or hayfields. The resounding bisyllabic, harshly croaking 'crex-crex', mostly heard at night, is so noisy and monotonous that it cannot be mistaken. Two or even three cocks can often be heard close together. A difficult bird to glimpse, but when flushed it wobbles through the air to the nearest cover with loosely-flapping wings and dangling legs. Its rust-coloured wings are a characteristic feature. A migrant, it arrives in April–May and leaves for Africa in August–September. Its numbers have declined in the west, but they have recently increased slightly in northern Europe.

Pheasant

Quail

Corncrake

Pheasant

juvenile about 15 days old

Quail

♂

♀

Corncrake

Baillon's crake *Porzana pusilla* 18 cm

A small crake, about the size of a house sparrow, and exceedingly difficult to see. The hen and cock are alike, but she is slightly duller with brown ear coverts. The courtship call is not as noisy as the little crake – audible from a distance of 200–250 m at most. Its dry scratchy sound, similar to the garganey, lasts for two or three seconds, fluctuating in volume. It is easily confused with the croaking of the edible frog. Baillon's crake inhabits rivers, mud flats, bogs, ponds and other – even very small – marshy areas with abundant vegetation, especially sedge. Its diet is the same as that of the little crake.

Little crake *Porzana parva* 19.5 cm

A shy bird, more easily spotted than Baillon's crake. The hen gives an overall pale impression with contrasting markings on her upper parts. Both sexes may be somewhat mottled and some (probably one-year-olds) look very lightly mottled. Feathers tend to become heavily worn during the summer. The little crake is muddy brown above, not chestnut, and lacks bars on its sides. Its legs are green and its bill base is red, features which distinguish it from Baillon's crake. The young resemble young Baillon's crakes, but their pale areas are blotches, not ring-shaped, arranged in rows to form light bars. Their wings are longer (adults, too) and the bars on their flanks may possibly be less conspicuous. The cock's call is a slow, low-pitched croaking, accelerating into a faster stammering 'quack .. quack .. quack .. quack, quack, quack, qua, qua, kva-kva-kva-kva-kva-kva'. The hen has a more vibrant closing trill which accelerates more rapidly, 'queck, queck, kverr'. Unlike other crakes, the little crake occurs in reed-beds where the water is fairly deep, and it is an accomplished swimmer. It lives on small aquatic creatures. Rare in western Europe.

Spotted crake *Porzana porzana* 23 cm

Hard to see. Usually looks dark, but if the light is good, it is easily recognizable by its spotted plumage, barred sides and buff under tail coverts. Its note is characteristic, a loud, resounding and rhythmically repeated, whistling 'whitt', only produced after dark. It occurs in fens, around lakes, ponds, rivers and in other places where there is shallow water and abundant vegetation, preferably osier and sedge. It lives on small aquatic creatures and plants.

Baillon's crake

Little crake

Spotted crake

Baillon's crake

♂

juvenile

juvenile

Little crake

♂ first year

♀

♂

Spotted crake

juvenile

Water rail *Rallus aquaticus* 28 cm

A solitary dark bird, larger than the crakes. Flies a short distance on loosely-flapping wings with legs dangling when alarmed. It is difficult to see, but patient quiet watching may reveal it standing openly on the edge of reeds, sunbathing, feeding or preening. More often, however, its presence is revealed by weird gruntings from deep in the vegetation: sudden, almost explosive outbursts or shrill pig-like squeals which are suddenly stifled and peter out into grunts, small whining 'quirr' noises and other rumble-tummy sound effects. On spring nights the cock produces a rhythmically hammering 'kupp ... kupp'. Reed-beds, fens, swamps and similar water plant jungles, including those interspersed with osier, are its habitat. Lives on small creatures, seeds and berries, and occasionally catches and kills other birds.

Moorhen *Gallinula chloropus* 33 cm

Unmistakable. Both walking and swimming it has a hen-like forward tilt, showing off its characteristic stern with ceaseless tail wagglings. Its wide repertoire of calls may be confusing on spring nights. A common one is a gurgling 'kurruck', another a repetitive 'keck'. Its display call, at night, is a persistently scolding 'kreck-kreck-kreck ...', sometimes emitted during extensive and unexpected night-time excursions on the wing. Sometimes shy, but usually – in park ponds, for instance – very bold. Found most often alone or in small groups on lakes, rivers or ponds where there is shelter in the reeds, bulrushes and osiers. Feeds on plant and animal matter – some taken from the surface, some by diving, and some from nearby fields.

Coot *Fulica atra* 40 cm

The coot is also unmistakable, although less skulking and usually more numerous than the moorhen, preferring larger, reed-fringed waters. Establishes a territory in early spring which it fiercely defends against encroachment, arching its wings high above its back like an angry swan. When taking off it runs across the water on long lobed toes, beating its wings. Typical calls are a loud, repetitive 'kock' and explosive, sometimes high-pitched 'pitts'. During nocturnal flights it also emits a somewhat hollow and desolate braying 'pe-auw'. Often seen in autumn and winter in close-knit flocks, grazing or diving for pondweed, plant stalks and small creatures.

Water rail

Moorhen

Coot

juvenile

Water rail

Moorhen

juvenile

juvenile

Coot

Crane *Grus grus*

114–130 cm, wing span 200–230 cm

A large majestic bird with a slow, measured, dignified tread on the ground. In flight it looks enormous, with long wings of even breadth, a thin neck outstretched (cf. the heron) and long projecting legs. In prolonged flight the approach is advertised by very loud notes consisting of nasal, jarring trumpet blasts. Surprisingly unobtrusive on its breeding grounds, the pair often call in a duet, 'krrui-krroh, krrui-krroh', especially at dawn. During spring, cranes perform a courtship dance in which they jump with wings raised, bow deeply, make trumpeting sounds and raise their 'plumes' (elongated inner secondaries). Breeding is in fairly small numbers in open or semi-open bogs and marshes. They migrate in family flocks, flying in V-formation or in a staggered line, dropping to rest in open farmland. They live on larger insects, small mammals and the occasional young bird, seeds and fruit.

Great bustard *Otis tarda*

♂ 102 cm ♀ 76 cm

The heaviest bird in Europe. Its size, the male's long throat feathers (only in breeding plumage) and the brownish bar across the breast develop gradually, with advancing age. A very shy bird, it walks, or rather saunters, with dignified steps and neck held high. Seen from a distance, a grazing flock is easily mistaken for sheep or other animals. Its flight is powerful, with steady wing beats and no gliding. The males perform a striking courtship display – an astonishing feat of apparently turning themselves inside-out into a large bundle of white feathers. Great bustards normally occur in large flocks in wide open farmland. Loss of habitat and the mechanization of farming have contributed towards their decline. Lives mainly on plants and seeds, but particularly in summer also eats insects, rodents and other small creatures which, when in good supply, are the main diet. The little bustard (*O. tetrax*) 43 cm breeds in the Mediterranean countries, France, north of the Black Sea and in central Asia. Instantly recognizable by its much smaller size.

Crane

Great bustard

Little bustard

juvenile

Crane

Great bustard

♂

♀

Waders and gulls *Charadriiformes*

Together with the auks, these two groups make up the order *Charadriiformes*.

Waders

A large group with about 35 species regularly occurring in northern Europe. Waders are divided into the following families: oystercatchers, plovers, stilts, avocets and a less uniform family (*Scolopacidae*) comprising snipe, curlews, sandpipers and small waders of the two subspecies *Calidris* and *Limicola*. Most of these are species which breed mainly in the Arctic but during their migration period can form a major ingredient of the fauna of many inland shores. The species included here breed beside lowland lakes and in fens and meadows south of the northern coniferous boundary and north of the Mediterranean countries. Species like redshank and little ringed plover also breed locally within this area. The wood sandpiper often occurs in numbers beside lowland lakes on autumn migration between July and October (see also the green sandpiper). The redshank (*Tringa totanus*) 28 cm is reminiscent of the wood sandpiper but is larger, has red legs and a striking white trailing wing edge. The little ringed plover (*Charadrius dubius*) 15 cm breeds on sandy and muddy shores, in gravel pits and where there are other similar soil structures. Its sister species, the ringed plover, has orange legs (not juveniles), white wing bars and does not have the yellow eye-ring. For further details see under the various species.

Redshank

Wood sandpiper

Little ringed plover

Gulls

Gulls are divided into skuas (family *Stercorariidae*) and gulls and terns (family *Laridae*). Some of the gull and tern species are characteristic residents of freshwater lakes. Gulls (subfamily *Larinae*) include a number of species such as the herring and black-headed gull. Each has a wide food spectrum and thus can be found in almost any surroundings. Adult plumages, mostly marked in white, grey and black, are preceded by a varying number of subadult stages. It takes the smaller species, such as the black-headed gull, about eighteen months, and the herring gull about four years, to develop adult plumage. There are often striking individual differences in moult, and a group of gulls often presents a motley appearance. Of the terns (subfamily *Sterninae*) – the species belonging to the family *Chlidonias* – field recognition may be difficult because of complex moulting patterns (cf. black tern). Apart from the black tern and the white-winged black tern, the whiskered tern (*C. hybrida*) occurs in southern Europe and central France. This bird, 24 cm long, resembles a black tern but is more heavily built and has a head like the common tern, with white cheeks and a black crown.

Black-headed gulls

Lapwings

Golden plover   *Pluvialis apricaria*   27 cm

Characterized by rounded contours, short bill, black markings on the underparts
and its manner. It moves jerkily, a few steps at a time, and then 'freezes' for a
second or two to contemplate its next step. The black markings vary and are con-
sistently less pronounced in the female, some of which have very few. Winter and
juvenile plumages are similar. The flight is straight and fast, and migrating birds
often fly in a blunt V-formation. Golden plovers are highly gregarious and often
seen in large flocks outside their breeding grounds. They will rest in ploughed fields,
on grazing land and in coastal meadows. They breed on moorlands. The flight
call is usually a plaintive melancholy 'puh' or 'pee'. Its display call is a repetitive
'plu-i-vie', sometimes followed by a faster rolling sound at the same pitch but with
'gravel' in its throat. Feeding habits are similar to the lapwing.

Lapwing   *Vanellus vanellus*   30 cm

The male's giddy wheeling flight on broad pied wings above ploughed fields in
March is a symbol of spring on northern farmland. The call of both sexes is a
snappy but soft 'pee-wit' during courtship or when alarmed. During the courtship
flight their wing beats are very noisy. When the pair are seen together in suitable
nesting fields, the brighter, more contrasting, colours of the male stand out clearly.
The female has a shorter crest, less distinct facial markings, and in rare cases a
completely black throat and a more greyish-green back. The juvenile resembles the
female in winter dress but has a grey breast. The migration pattern is complex,
some birds moving away in winter, others staying, while young birds disperse to
all points of the compass. Outside the breeding season large flocks congregate on
farmland and marshes, often with golden plovers. The lapwing lives on insects,
worms and vegetable food.

Golden plover

Lapwing

juvenile

Golden plover

♂

♂

Lapwing

♂

♀ winter

Common sandpiper   *Tringa hypoleucos*   20 cm

Common, and often the only wader on many freshwater lakes and rivers. Recognizable by its repeated needle-sharp and piercing 'hee-dee-dee' as it takes to the wing. Its flight is then very distinctive: a mouse-coloured bird with a long tail and white wing bars skimming fast and low over the water. Its wings vibrate rapidly, alternating with short glides on downturned wings. A favourite posture is standing on stones, and the constantly bobbing tail is a characteristic feature. Its courtship call is a fast, monotonous sequence of sharp 'pipitividih-pipitividih ...', sounds often heard throughout the day. The warning note is a piercing and persistent 'hiip'. For breeding, it selects a tuft of grass preferably close to stony or muddy shores without dense marshland vegetation but overshadowed by trees. During migration it sometimes pauses by very small pools or drainage ditches. Lives mainly on insects and other invertebrates.

Green sandpiper   *Tringa ochropus*   23 cm

A dark-backed, nervous and very unobtrusive sandpiper. In flight there is a striking contrast between dark wide wings and back and the white rump and belly. Juvenile birds have a darker crown and neck and small ochre spots on their upper parts. The bird occasionally bobs its tail. On migration it occurs singly or in twos and threes beside small ponds and ditches, preferably muddy ones. May be confused with the wood sandpiper (*T. glareola*) 21 cm which, however, is more slender, paler overall, and has narrower wings which are paler beneath. The green sandpiper's call is a snappy 'twi't-vit-vit', the wood sandpiper's being a softer 'chiff-iff-iff'. Its courtship song is a stream of yodelling whistles, 'tluitiht-tluitiht ...' and its warning call a hammering 'titt-titt-titt ...'. The female may migrate south as early as the beginning of June, having returned to the breeding grounds as soon as the ice breaks. Same diet as the common sandpiper.

Terek sandpiper   *Xenus cinereus*

(see picture p. 76)
23 cm

A wader the size of a green sandpiper, although posture and flight are the same as the common sandpiper. Recognizable by the long upward-curved bill, steep forehead, drab plumage with a black V on its back, partially visible black wing 'shoulders' and short yellow-grey legs (yellow in winter dress). In flight, the pale grey trailing-edges of the wings are as striking as those of the redshank. Call variable, usually a fast 'chu-du-du' or a rolling 'trurrrut' on the wing. Exceedingly rare in western Europe, even on migration.

Common sandpiper

Green sandpiper

Terek sandpiper

Common sandpiper

Green sandpiper

Green sandpiper

Common sandpiper

winter

Terek sandpiper

(see text p. 74)

Ruff *Philomachus pugnax* ♂ 30 cm ♀ 24 cm

An extraordinary wader, but may be mistaken, in its more anonymous plumages, for other species. During May and June the ruffs (males), which are considerably larger than the reeves (females), carry conspicuous 'ear'-tufts, ruffs and other multicoloured feathers and facial 'wattles'. This infinitely variable plumage can be confusing. Young birds, which outnumber adults during autumn migration, vary from yellowish grey to brownish red. Winter plumage resembles the juvenile but is a drabber grey. The flight is an exaggerated pigeon-like flapping of the wings, and gliding is common. During May and June the ruffs congregate on special arenas in their breeding grounds – wet meadows and fenlands – for the courtship ceremonies or 'lekks'. They dance, or rather buffet each other, with ruffs extended, wings flapping, jumping, bowing and trailing their wings on the ground to attract a reeve. During migration they pause beside muddy pools and estuaries, and in waterlogged meadows, but will also rest and feed in fields. They live on small creatures, but during the winter in Africa mainly eat seeds.

Ruff

Ruff

♂

juvenile

♂ summer

♀ summer

Black-tailed godwit

Curlew

Black-tailed godwit   *Limosa limosa*   40–44 cm

A lanky wader, easily recognizable by its size, colour and, above all, conspicuous appearance in flight. The summer plumage varies. The male is often more colourful and reddish tinged than the female, who sometimes appears during the nesting season in an almost 'winter' plumage (see picture). Juveniles have colour markings like young ruffs. The bar-tailed godwit (*L. lapponica*), a species breeding in the Arctic, is similar but only rarely seen inland. It lacks the white on wing and tail feathers. The black-tailed godwit is a noisy bird on its breeding grounds, with various nasal and nervously reiterated sounds such as 'vivivi' or 'ke-vecka', a longer, vibrant 'krrreeuu', or, when alarmed, a rapid 'ki-vi-vi'. Courtship is an equally noisy procedure, as one or a few males display with a rapid wheeling flight and fast, vibrant wing beats. Breeding grounds are wet meadows and marshes close to water. Food is found by probing soil or mud with the sensitive beak which the bird scratches to keep the tip clean. Coastal in winter.

Curlew   *Numenius arquata*   56–63 cm

The largest European wader. Common and widely known but shy and well camouflaged against a moorland background. The sexes are similar (although the male is smaller and slimmer) and juveniles are very like adults. In spring the males display over farmland, meadows and moorland, corkscrewing into the sky on flapping wings before parachuting down with wings bent like a gull. Initially crooning, the song accelerates into a trill and then bubbles over into brilliant moorland music. The deeply resonant fluting tone is also noticeable in the call, a soft 'koi' or 'kloyit'. The curlew can be confused with the very similar whimbrel (*N. phaeopus*) 43–47 cm, which mainly breeds in mountain and tundra regions, but has bold snipe-like crown markings and a less tuneful bubbling trill. The curlew lives on insects, worms, snails, small creatures and various vegetable foods. Coastal in winter.

Black-tailed godwit

Curlew

Black-tailed godwit ♂

♀

Curlew ♂

Snipe

Snipe *Gallinago gallinago* 27 cm

The only one of the three European snipe species to breed outside the mountain and tundra regions. Common in summer on fenland, wet meadows and marshes, it is also seen during migration on muddy shores and creeks. It seeks its food – worms and insects – by probing mud and loose soil with very jerky bill movements. There is thus a somewhat mechanical look about the bird. It crouches motionless when in danger, and in the water may stay two-thirds submerged below the surface. It takes to the wing explosively with rapid wing beats when the intruder is a few metres away, and zig-zags from side to side, calling a hoarse 'ketch'. The courtship flight alternates between flappy climbs and dives, with the vibration of the outer tail feathers making a characteristic loud drumming. Its mating call is a loud rhythmic 'tick-a, tick-a . . .', sometimes delivered from a pole. It is active at night.

Stone curlew *Burhinus oedicnemus* 42 cm

The odd-man-out among the birds of Europe, with its large head, glaring eyes and often motionless posture. Found in small numbers in arid areas and in cereal fields, and is nearly always encountered in camouflage-coloured, rather desiccated stony and shrubby ground. It 'freezes', crouches low or runs away rather than taking to the wing. When frightened it flies only a short distance, keeping close to the ground with fast shallow wing beats. The bold wing marking is unmistakable in flight. The flight call is a 'kui', 'krrui-lii' of varying loudness. On the ground it has a wide repertoire of calls, including a rapidly repeated 'kurr-ri, kurr-ri . . .', a rather oystercatcher-ish 'kruvit, kruvit . . .' and a clear 'viip'. Mainly active at dusk and during the night, it lives on snails, insects and worms and can even catch and eat rather large animals such as mice, nestlings and frogs.

Snipe

Stone curlew

Snipe

drumming

Stone curlew

Little gull   *Larus minutus*   30 cm

Easily overlooked among colonies of black-headed gulls where it often breeds. It is smaller than the black-headed, however, and its flight is lighter, often dipping down to the water surface like the black tern. The rounder wings of the adults are completely dark underneath and grey, framed in white, on top. In summer the head is pitch-black, not chocolate brown, while the winter plumage looks like the black-headed. On the rare occasions when it is seen perched, it is strikingly short in the leg and looks like a tern. Juveniles acquire a grey mantle in autumn, and grey head and neck markings. The characteristic juvenile wing markings, however, are retained until they are about one year old (see picture). The calls are most often a repetitive, harsh, tern-like 'chee-eh-check-check', or a nasal 'euv'. The display call is a whining 'ke-veu, ke-veu, ke-veu . . .' similar to the black-tailed godwit. In courtship flight the male stretches his neck and flies with deep wing beats; sometimes several males will 'butterfly' display in close formation. The little gull breeds beside shallow, often eutrophic, lakes but winters at sea. It catches insects on the wing or snaps up other food from the water surface.

Black-headed gull   *Larus ridibundus*   38–44 cm

Easily recognized in flight in all plumages by the white leading-edge and black trailing-edge of the primaries. In winter the white head has a dark ear patch, while legs and bill base are a paler red. First winter plumage has a grey mantle (see p. 88). Widespread and numerous, with an increasing distribution area in recent years. Adaptable as to food and habitat and commonly seen beside fresh water, on the seashore, on recently ploughed farmland, often together with common gulls, and in town centres. Breeds in colonies, often large, and often beside reed-fringed lakes. Its distinctive calls are raucous and ear-splitting and thus hard to transcribe.

Little gull

Black-headed gull

juvenile

Little gull

first year

juvenile

Black-headed gull

juvenile

Common gulls

Common gull *Larus canus* 41–45 cm

Similar to the herring gull but smaller, slimmer and more fluent in its movements, with a gentler face and, invariably, a much thinner bill. Juveniles moult in autumn and acquire partly or completely grey mantles. In spring the body feathers are shed once again and the wings bleach, so that in May or June a year-old common gull often looks very pale, almost floury white (see p. 88). The calls are brighter than the herring gull, usually a nasal and indistinct 'kiew', which can be prolonged into a bright melodious 'caowee' or a cackling 'ke-ke-ke ...'. The alarm call is an insistent 'gliu-gliu ...'. Breeds inland in small colonies, or occasionally singly, beside lakes and large rivers, although not in shallow lowland eutrophic lakes. Quite often it breeds in fields far from water. A frequent visitor to grassland, particularly after rain, but also follows the plough to find worms and insects. Its diet also includes small fish, other water creatures and the occasional bird's egg.

Herring gull *Larus argentatus* 58–67 cm

For differences between herring and common gull, see above. Full plumage does not develop until about the fourth winter, and subadult appearance varies a great deal. The grey mantle is usually acquired by the second winter (often with a few brown-marked feathers). Populations or races outside western Scandinavia and central and western Europe have yellowish legs. The mellow calls include prolonged 'aou', frequently repeated, and a scolding alarm call 'ag-ag-ag ...'. It breeds inland beside large lakes. Often seen flying over cultivated areas, and now nests on buildings in some places. Migrates in a V-formation. Omnivorous, and in winter frequents refuse tips.

Common gull

Herring gull

juvenile

Common gull

Herring gull

Common tern   *Sterna hirundo*   36–42 cm

In much of Europe this is the only black-crested tern breeding near fresh water. The Arctic tern (*S. paradisaea*) only breeds on the coast and beside clear lakes and rivers in northern Scandinavia and Britain. The young may be confused with black terns in juvenile or winter plumage, but they have an orange bill base and a less flappy flight. The calls are hoarse and rattling: a short harsh 'kik' or a prolonged 'keee-yaaah'. Often breeds in colonies beside all types of fresh water and on the coast. It dives for fish, insects and other water creatures.

Black tern   *Chlidonias niger*   24 cm

Its flight, like a big lazy swallow, attracts attention as it moves above vegetation looking for flying insects. Note the flying style because in a strong backlight it is difficult to judge the range of dark colours of different tern species. Sometimes the head and underparts do not turn black until spring, and autumn moult begins early, from June onwards, so that individual plumages may appear piebald. Not vociferous, but the commonest calls are a nasal 'cheh' and a short 'chick'. Breeds colonially beside shallow, eutrophic lowland lakes and marshes. In many areas its numbers have declined, due mostly to drainage. Migration is as early as July or August, mostly along the coast to tropical Africa.

White-winged black tern   *Chlidonias leucopterus*   24 cm

A bird with highly contrasting markings, the brilliant white wings make flight look more graceful as it dances weightlessly in slow motion. Individuals vary greatly in the contrasts of their upper parts: some look almost like a black tern, especially in backlighting. In doubtful cases, however, the bird is almost certainly a black tern; the snow-white leading-edges of the white-winged stand out clearly among a flock of black terns. In winter and juvenile plumages it differs from the black tern by the absence of a dark patch on the breast at the front of the wing, and also by the broader white leading-edge, its smaller dark head marking and, in juveniles, a dark mantle. Notice, too, the pale grey (not white) rump and tail in juvenile and winter plumage, although with white outer tail feathers (cf. black tern p. 89). Its calls are harsher, a 'keck', 'krreck' or a short 'kick'. Otherwise its habits and behaviour are similar to those of the black tern, but it is more selective in its choice of habitat.

Common tern   Black tern   White-winged black tern

Common tern

Arctic tern

White-winged black tern

Black tern

Common gull
first year

Herring gull
first year (May)

Common gull
second year
summer

Black-headed gull

summer
first year

Lesser black-backed gull

Lesser black-backed gull (*Larus fuscus*) 53–59 cm. There are two species in Europe
– *fuscus* in the Baltic countries, has soot-black upper parts, and *graellsii*, with dark
grey upper parts, in western Europe. Their legs are yellow. Found on the coasts
and, particularly in Finland and the Baltic countries, on inland lakes. A migrant
mainly in western Europe but also occurs in northern Europe.

juvenile

White-winged
black tern

winter

juvenile

Black tern

winter

first year

juvenile

Common tern

Barn owl *Tyto alba* 35 cm

More often heard than seen because of its nocturnal habits. Pale, almost white, when seen in the light of car headlights or a street lamp. This is particularly true of the race (*alba*) found in western and southern Europe, which is paler than the northeastern one (*guttata*). The wings in flight are proportionally shorter and the head larger than the short-eared owl. The territorial call is a prolonged piercing shriek, the warning call a faster, razor-sharp shriek. Appearance, calls and its habit of visiting and nesting in barns, old warehouses, ruins and towers give it a rather ghostly personality. Occurs principally in open farmland, feeding mainly on small rodents.

Short-eared owl *Asio flammeus* 37 cm

Usually active during the day, but hunts mostly at dusk and early morning, and thus is fairly easily spotted. Characteristically, it perches on a mound or post and the deep black cavities surrounding brilliant yellow eyes give it a rather demonic appearance. The small 'ears' are only raised in alarm. In flight the long wings move jerkily and stiffly, but it glides elegantly and with great agility. The wings are very pale underneath and the feathers translucent, with a striking dark crescent-shaped patch at the 'elbows' and dark bars on the tips. The similar long-eared owl (*Asio otus*) 35 cm is a forest or woodland bird but hunts in open country. Its flight resembles the short-eared, but its wings are shorter with different markings. The short-eared owl breeds on the ground in wide open spaces such as moors, bogs, marshes and rough grassland. Because it feeds mainly on small rodents, the numbers and breeding success of the birds are largely governed by their availability. The male's note is a dull pumping 'do-do-do-do-do' and the female's a hoarse 'tchehhh-opp'.

Barn owl

Short-eared owl

Long-eared owl

race *guttata*

race *alba*

Barn owl

Short-eared owl

Little owl *Athene noctua*   23 cm

This bird is usually easy to identify because in many areas of Europe it is the only owl of its size that is active in the day-time, looking like a brownish-grey, squat lump atop a telegraph pole, roof or a fence pole. If it is surprised when perching, usually low in a tree, during the day, it may move a short distance in deeply undulating flight. It hops easily on the ground but adopts a more upright posture when alarmed and bobs almost like a robin. Tengmalm's owl (*Aegolius funereus*), which is similar in appearance, occurs only in the forests of northern and highland central Europe. The scops owl (*Otus scops*), found in southern Europe, is smaller and more angular, has distinct ear tufts and is active only at night. The territorial call of the little owl is a prolonged puppy-like yelp on a rising scale. Other calls are a softer 'kiiu', and an agitated 'kip-kip-kip ...' when alarmed. The young have a begging 'hsss'. The little owl occurs in open woodland, farmland with trees, towns with parks or large gardens, and nests in holes in trees, buildings or even cliffs. It lives on rodents, small birds, insects, worms and snails.

Swift *Apus apus*   17 cm

The sole representative of the order *Apodiformes* in northern Europe. Distinguished from the swallows by its all-dark plumage and narrower sickle-shaped wings which – unlike those of the swallows and martins – are always held stiffly at right angles to the body in flight. Adaptation to life in the air is so complete that swifts are seen in most surroundings. When feeding they are found in large numbers over lowland lakes, reservoirs and marshes. Breeds mostly in colonies in towns, under roof tiles and in holes in buildings. Insect food is caught in flight by scooping with the wide mouth. During extensive foraging trips the swift collects a marble-sized ball of food in its throat. Feeding depends entirely on weather that is suitable for flying insects: swifts travel hundreds of kilometres to avoid poor weather conditions. Young birds are uniquely adapted to this way of life; after a few days' short rations they lapse into a torpid energy-saving state which allows them to survive ten to fifteen days' starvation (during which period their growth is suspended). Groups of swifts often fly 'in formation' at tremendous speed around their breeding grounds and over roofs, emitting rolling piercing screams, often in unison with the birds beneath the roof tiles. Migration is between July and September, with return in May or June.

Little owl

Swift

Little owl

Swift   juvenile   adult with food-ball in throat

Kingfisher

Dipper

Kingfisher *Alcedo atthis* 18 cm

Despite, or perhaps because of, its colouring, the kingfisher is difficult to see. Often one can only glimpse the glitter of its pale turquoise back. Most often its call attracts attention: a piercing and very distinctive harsh 'ziii' or 'zrii'. Its rapid flight with whirring wing beats is interspersed with short glides. It fishes from a branch, stick or other strategic position overhanging the water, but it can also hover. It frequents clear and fast-flowing rivers, preferably where there are willow or alder branches over the water, but occasionally may also be seen near ponds and small ditches, and even on the coast. It breeds in sand or earth banks, where it excavates a tunnel up to a metre in length. Its diet is fish and water insects.

Dipper *Cinclus cinclus* 18 cm

Found on fast-flowing waters, the dipper prefers stony rapids in streams, but in winter it also frequents slower-moving rivers. In its usual habitat of stones and a mixture of dark and sparkling water, the bird blends completely with its surroundings. The flat black dipper gives itself away with sharp, piercing, somewhat rasping 'stritts', simultaneously speeding close to the water on buzzing wings. At regular intervals it plunges into the rapids, dives to the bottom and, using its short wings as fins, looks for insect larvae, molluscs and fish eggs. Mission accomplished, it pops up to the surface to take a breather, floating along for a short distance, wings outspread, before again rising into the air. Its song is a subdued collection of whistling and squeaking phrases. The British race has more chestnut on the belly (see picture) than the continental.

Kingfisher ♂

Dipper

juvenile

Perching birds *Passeriformes*

The largest order, by far, in numbers of both individuals and species. Sizes and habits vary greatly, but one common feature of all passerines is the combination of three toes pointing forward and one to the rear. In addition to species directly associated with fenland and lakeside vegetation (reed warbler and bearded reedling), there are others that can usually be found in these surroundings (starlings and tits, for example). Farmland is also frequented by starlings, several thrush species, several finches, buntings and sparrows. Knowledge of the various families is a great help in the identification of perching birds. The following are found in Europe.

Larks (*Alaudidae*) which live on the ground, are camouflaged and stoutly built and have thick bills. **Swallows** (*Hirundinidae*) are skilful fliers, and feed on insects caught on the wing. They often perch on telegraph wires and frequently spend the night among common reeds. **Wagtails** and **pipits** (*Motacillidae*) are graceful and long-legged with relatively long tails. **Shrikes** (*Laniidae*), **orioles** (*Oriolidae*), **starlings** (*Sturnidae*) and **waxwings** (*Bombycillidae*) are similar in size and shape, but varied in colour, food and behaviour. **Crows** (*Corvidae*) are the largest of the perching birds. Stout-billed and mostly omnivorous, their main markings are black, grey and white. **Dippers** (*Cinclidae*) are semi-aquatic; wrens (*Troglodytidae*) and **accentors** (*Prunellidae*) feed deep in vegetation. The **warblers** (*Sylviidae*) are an extensive group of small, often nondescript, mainly insectivorous birds that move swiftly in vegetation and are most easily identified by their song. They inhabit a wide variety of surroundings. In this group the *Locustella* and *Acrocephalus* families are most commonly found in wetlands, although species such as the willow warbler, chiffchaff and blackcap are often attracted by the abundant insect life of reeds and osier beds, especially during migration. The whitethroat breeds in scrub, sometimes on the edges of cultivated fields. **Cetti's warbler** (*Cettia cetti*) is a southern European wetland species which has spread northwards in western Europe and now reaches as far as southern England. It is unobtrusive, difficult to spot, and dark with dull brown upper parts, and grey underparts. Its heavily-rounded tail constantly flicks. The characteristic song is an explosive bubbling tirade of loud clear notes. **Flycatchers** (*Muscicapidae*) catch insects on the wing. **Thrushes** (*Turdidae*) are another extensive group which includes true thrushes, wheatears, chats, bluethroats, nightingales and robins. Most of these species have a perky upright stance. Of the **bearded reedlings** (*Timaliidae*), **penduline tits** (*Remizidae*) and **titmice** (*Paridae*), the titmice live mainly in forests, woodland and gardens, but blue tits often venture into reeds in autumn and winter to dig insects and insect larvae. Of the **nuthatches** (*Sittidae*), **creepers** (*Certhidae*) and **weavers** (*Ploceidae*), two representatives, the house sparrow and tree sparrow, are common on agricultural land. **Finches** (*Fringillidae*) are similar to buntings but have shorter tails and are more compactly built. Several, such as chaffinch, brambling, greenfinch and linnet feed in the same way as sparrows. **Buntings** (*Emberizidae*) inhabit swamps, open woodland, arable land and reed-fringed lakes. Their plumage is equally variable but they often all have the typical beak with larger lower mandible.

Skylark

Meadow pipit

House sparrow ♀

Linnet ♀

juvenile
autumn

Wheatear ♀

Corn bunting

Bearded reedling ♀

Sand martin

Reed warbler

Rook

Penduline tit
juvenile

Skylark *Alauda arvensis*   18 cm

Hard to spot on the ground because of its camouflage. Plumage tone varies widely
from pale sandy beige to some of the brownish-red (recently moulted) individuals
seen in autumn. Sometimes looks fat, sometimes slender and rather like a pipit.
Often raises its crown feathers to form a crest, never quite so impressively as the
crested lark. In an undulating flight flappy wing beats alternate with glides, and
the white trailing-edges of the wings are clearly visible. Vociferous on the wing,
uttering various 'chirrups'. Its song is unmistakable, a ceaseless flow of trills and
yodellings, often interspersed with imitative noises, and the performance may take
place in an almost hovering flight at a considerable altitude, or else from a perch.
Frequents open grassland and farmland, and lives on various plant materials and
small terrestrial invertebrates.

Woodlark *Lullula arborea*   15 cm

Distinguished by its strikingly short tail and pale tips to its lesser and primary coverts.
White-tipped tail, without white outer feathers, is visible in flight, which is slow
and bouncy, with flapping wing beats alternating with periods of complete wing
retraction. Its call is a pleasant flutey 'tuetli-oit', and its song is also a soft fluting
descending yodel. The woodlark is found on moorland, sandy scrub and in thinly-
wooded farming country. Its diet is the same as that of the skylark but with a
larger proportion of insects.

Crested lark *Galerida cristata*   17 cm

The long crest and stout bill are outstanding features. In flight its short tail shows
rust red at the edges and it moves its broad wings gently and loosely. When taking
to the air it usually emits a 'du-i', and often uses a variable, soft fluting 'tui-tuu-tioo',
similar to the woodlark. Its song is slower and usually of a clearer timbre than
the skylark's, but it does not have the skylark's habit of repeating long sequences,
although it intertwines its song with imitative sounds. Sings from an exposed perch
or stone, but will also execute a song flight at low height. In northern Europe
(except Britain and Ireland) the crested lark is something of a 'back-garden bird',
because it likes bare areas along embankments, railway lines, warehouses and derelict
areas. Its feeding habits are similar to the skylark's but with fewer insects.

Skylark

Woodlark

Crested lark

Skylark

juvenile

Woodlark

Crested lark

Swallow *Hirundo rustica* 19–22 cm

Adult birds can be easily recognized by their elongated outer tail feathers (slightly shorter in the female). In juveniles, during autumn, these feathers are only about 1 cm long. Juveniles are more beige than chestnut on the forehead and throat, and have a greyish-brown bar on the breast. The note is a tinkling, cheerful 'vitt' or 'vitt vitt'. The song is a persistent crystal-clear twittering intertwined with imitative sounds which are sometimes rounded off with a typical 'oil-that-hinge' creaking. The swallow is commonest near villages and farms. Large flocks assemble during migration, together with martins and swifts, above fens and reed-fringed lakes where there are plentiful airborne insects. They roost in reed-beds. The cup-shaped nest made of mud pellets is built under eaves, on roof beams and in niches inside barns and outbuildings. Migrates to southern Africa.

House martin *Delichon urbica* 14.5 cm

The white rump is easily spotted. In autumn juveniles are darkly shaded on the sides of their breast making them look like sand martins when seen from the front. The house martin's call is a bright but scratchy 'prrit'. Its song, usually performed from a telephone wire, is a yodelling variation on the same theme. House martins breed in colonies on buildings and cliffs and occur over a wide variety of habitats, often close to water but not necessarily close to human settlement. Although food is caught at a higher altitude, their diet resembles that of the swallow.

Sand martin *Riparia riparia* 13.5 cm

The bar across its breast and dull brown upper parts make the sand martin easily recognizable. The dry rasping call is a characteristic. It breeds in colonies in holes dug out of the sand, usually in sand-pits or river banks, and for this reason its distribution is limited. It often feeds over rivers, ponds and lowland lakes, and like other swallow species catches insects and spiders in flight. Often skims over water, drinking as it flies, or bathes by dunking itself in the surface. Usually double-brooded. From midsummer onwards large gatherings can be seen, especially around overnight roosts in reed-beds. Throughout the autumn juvenile birds are in light scaly plumage. Sand martins winter in tropical Africa.

Swallow

House martin

Sand martin

Sand martin House martin Swallow

House martin
juvenile

House martin

Swallow

juvenile

Sand martin

House martin

House martin   juvenile

Tree pipit *Anthus trivialis*   15 cm

Associated with woodland, but rests on grassland or by lake shores when migrating.
As with other pipits, the call is its most important trade-mark – a hoarse 'pizzt'
or 'buzzt' on take-off or in flight. Among the characteristics that mark its differences from the meadow pipit are more blurred and somewhat watered-down dark
back markings, distinct pale areas between moustache and cheek, the slightly longer
and heavier body and upper parts that are more greyish in spring.

Meadow pipit *Anthus pratensis*   14.5 cm

One of the commonest perching birds in open country, but is often inconspicuous.
Usually takes to the wing about ten metres ahead of the observer, hovers in the
air for a moment with wings fluttering, and then emits a persistent 'psit, psit ...
psit' call before making a jerky descent into the grass again. When not alarmed,
meadow pipits keep in touch with each other with a chirping 'chutt' or 'chitt'.
They also have a bright ringing 'tisitsi', like the dunnock's note, and a rough
'ch-tt utt utt utt ...'. The warning call is a persistent 'stitt-itt'. The song is divided
into fast accelerating 'tsip' sounds, thinner, more prolonged 'tsuht' sounds and
a whirring trill, usually in that order. This is performed in a song flight, rising
first and then slowly descending on spread wings like a parachute. Open grassland,
arable farmland and moorland are breeding areas and waterlogged land and lakesides
are frequent haunts. The diet is small invertebrate animals.

Red-throated pipit *Anthus cervinus*   14.5 cm

A migrant to northeastern Europe, very rare elsewhere, wintering in central and
eastern Africa. Although the habitat is similar to the meadow pipit, its call is almost
invariably revealing. It produces a single, protracted, sharp and sometimes slightly
hoarse 'spiiih', or occasionally 'spuuuh'. The colours and patterns of underparts
vary greatly in spring, and many individuals are pale with only a suggestion of
red. All the year round, however, the red-throated is distinguishable from the
meadow pipit by clearer markings on its back and flanks. The heavy rump markings,
however, are often hard to see in the field.

Tree pipit

Meadow pipit

Red-throated pipit

Tree pipit
autumn

Meadow pipit

juvenile
autumn

autumn

Meadow pipit

summer

autumn

summer

Red-throated pipit

Tawny pipit   *Anthus campestris*   16.5 cm

The larger size and very pale, almost unstreaked, sandy-coloured plumage is immediately recognizable. Individuals, however, may have fairly distinct streaks on
the breast. In autumn the upper parts are a darker brownish grey, and in some
young birds the retention of juvenile feathers creates distinctly patchy underparts.
The tawny may be confused with the East Asian Richard's pipit (*A. novaeseelandiae*)
18 cm, which can very occasionally be seen in open country in Europe during September and October, especially on coast marshland. Richard's pipit, however, is
the size of a skylark, with clear streaks on breast and mantle and a characteristic,
widely audible and hoarse call, 'r-r-ripp'. The first winter plumage of the female
yellow wagtail could be confused with the tawny pipit's, but she probably always
has a dash of yellow on her belly or beneath her tail. Tawny pipit calls are many
and varied, including a protracted 'tsiip', a dunnock-like 'tschilp' and a short,
reiterated 'chup'. The song is a slowly repeated, melancholy, metallic 'ziryh', with
a rolling towards the end, produced either during a characteristic song flight of
a long, deep-curving trajectory, or from an exposed perch. The tawny pipit breeds
in dry heath country with thin vegetation and patches of bare soil or sand, preferably
interspersed with trees or bushes. Elsewhere it colonizes clear-felled woodland and
even desiccated farmland, feeding mostly on insects.

White/pied wagtail   *Motacilla alba*   18 cm

The only wagtail with exclusively black and white markings, although after their
moult in September–October many individuals have a touch of yellow over the
white, while young birds may have some olive green above the grey. All markings
are extremely variable during the autumn. In spring the female's grey neck merges
into a black crown. Britain and Ireland and neighbouring continental coasts are
the breeding grounds of the race *yarellii*, the pied wagtail, which has areas of darker
grey or black. The adult male has all-black upper parts and flanks which are not
always visible. In the autumn, however, young birds and some females are indistinguishable from the continental race *alba*. The call is a snappy mellifluous 'chiss-
zick'. The song is rather agitated and twittery, with phrases resembling the call.
White or pied wagtails occur in many habitats but prefer open sunlit areas with
plenty of insects. They often nest near water, in cavities under bridges, on river
banks, jetties or buildings, even in town centres.

Tawny pipit

White/pied wagtail

juvenile

Tawny pipit ♂

race *alba*
summer

White/pied
wagtail

race *yarellii*
winter

juvenile
autumn

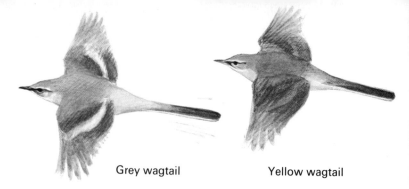

Grey wagtail   Yellow wagtail

Grey wagtail *Motacilla cinerea* 18 cm

Often frequents fast-running water and sometimes appears side by side with the dipper near waterfalls and rapids in stony streams. Differs from the yellow wagtail in that it has a much longer tail, completely grey back and darker wings. In young females during autumn, only the under tail coverts are yellow. The long tail and white wing bar are conspicuous in the deeply undulating flight. A nimble and elegant bird and an expert at chasing insects among stones, its tail seems to wag perpetually whenever it stands still. The call resembles the white wagtail's but is sharper and higher pitched, a 'stitt' or 'zti-titt'. Sequences of notes resembling its call make up the song.

Yellow wagtail *Motacilla flava* 16.5 cm

Several yellow wagtail races breed in Europe, and all have fairly distinct head markings. The race *flava* breeds in most of central and northern Europe, *flavissima* (female similar to the male but much paler) in the British Isles, and *thunbergi* (like *flava* but with blacker ear coverts and lacking the white eyebrow) in northern Scandinavia and the USSR. Birds migrating in autumn, which appear in large numbers during August and September, display a great variety of plumages, but the shorter tail, the paler edges to the wing coverts and the greyish-brown back always distinguish them from the grey wagtail. Their calls are pleasant, the commonest being a protracted 'zieh', a slightly rolling 'zrrie', a bright ringing 'zi-si-si' or a short repeated 'psit'. The song is a rather chirrupy ditty most often performed with a puffed-out chest (see picture). The yellow wagtail is a bird of damp meadows and marshland, breeding in tussocky grasses. In autumn it often frequents grazing land, using sheep and horses as beaters to stir up its insect food.

Grey wagtail

Yellow wagtail

Grey wagtail ♀

race *flava* ♂

race *flavissima* ♂

juvenile ♀ autumn

race *flava*

race *flava* ♀ autumn Yellow wagtail

Hooded crow   Rook

Carrion crow   *Corvus corone*   47 cm

The hooded and carrion crows are races of the same species and can produce hybrids
with varied plumage patterns. The carrion crow (*corone*) is easily confused with
young rooks (see below) and perhaps even with the jackdaw (*Corvus monedula*)
33 cm, which also occurs in fields and meadows. The jackdaw, however, is much
smaller, with a grey neck and a characteristic white iris. Crows occur in many
habitats, often in ones or twos, as large flocks are less usual than in the rook.
Food is found in fields and ploughed land, but during spring and summer birds'
eggs and nestlings make up a considerable proportion of its omnivorous diet. Thus
lowland lakes, with large bird populations, generally have a few resident pairs.

Rook   *Corvus frugileus*   47 cm

The rook is more often seen on cultivated farmland than the crow, feeding in fields
of short grass or cereals. Its rolling gait, peaked forehead and long pale beak (the
bald base makes the bill look long) and the baggy 'trousers' around its legs are
characteristic features. Young birds, however, are often astonishingly hard to distinguish from the carrion crows, because until they are about a year old they have
a dark brush of feathers over the 'nose'. The forehead shape is always different,
however, and the rook's wing, like the rest of its plumage, is rather loosely con-
structed – the bastard wing and the primary coverts, for example, often droop slightly.
The call is more nasal and higher pitched than the crow's. The rook's diet is equally
divided between various animal and vegetable foods.

Hooded crow   Carrion crow   Rook

Hooded crow

Carrion crow

juvenile

Rook

Savi's warbler   *Locustella luscinoides*   14 cm

Distinguished from grasshopper and river warblers by plumage – more like the reed warbler's – and choice of habitat. It is less retiring than the grasshopper warbler, but jerky movements, cocked tail and tendency to 'fall' into the undergrowth when in danger all distinguish it from marsh and reed warblers. Savi's warblers occur in lush waterside vegetation, especially in *Phragmites*. Perched on a reed, it sings a song resembling the grasshopper warbler's but is faster, lower pitched, a mechanical ratchet-like buzzing. It seems to sing more readily and in daylight often executes short phrases, although at night it may sing continuously. The call is a staccato 'pitch', and when alarmed it produces a harsh chattering.

River warbler   *Locustella fluviatilis*   13.5 cm

The river warbler, an eastern species, is distinguished from grasshopper and Savi's warblers by its unstreaked greyish-brown upper parts and streaked breast. It also has unusually long lower tail coverts with pale tips. A shy bird, it is usually located by its song, as persistent and mechanical as the grasshopper warbler's, but slower and more like a sewing machine 'zezezezeze . . .', with the syllables clearly articulated. The song perch is usually higher than the grasshopper warbler's, near the top of an osier bush, alder or willow, 2–4 m above the ground. The river warbler is encountered in waterlogged woodlands, alder thickets and osier beds bordering on rivers. (See also Cetti's warbler, p. 96.)

Grasshopper warbler   *Locustella naevia*   13 cm

A small warbler, exceedingly hard to spot as it creeps in the undergrowth, detectable only because of its song. If flushed it will fly jerkily away for a short distance, looking dark olive brown, and with a rounded tail. Although unobtrusive it is not in the least shy, and sometimes displays curiosity when clambering up the stalks of plants, cocking its tail regularly (a typical trait of the *Locustella* species). Sometimes it produces a harsh 'stitt', but its song is a monotonous insect-like buzzing which, with short intermissions, continues for hours. It sings from low in a bush, and its most intensive performances are at dawn and dusk. Favours lush vegetation usually bordering wetlands but occasionally in quite dry scrub, and feeds on insects.

Savi's warbler

River warbler

Grasshopper warbler

110–111

Savi's warbler

River warbler

Grasshopper warbler

Blyth's reed warbler *Acrocephalus dumetorum* 12.5 cm

A northeastern European bird, rare elsewhere. Apart from its song, it is hard to distinguish from the marsh warbler, but the wings appear shorter and, as a rule, legs and beak are darker. The tuneful song differs from the marsh warbler's in its steady tempo, distinct pauses and the repetition of each phrase several times, like a song thrush. It is a first-class mimic. The song could be confused with an Icterine warbler's. Vocalizes mainly at night, often perched 3–5 m above the ground in a bush or tree, sometimes sitting on a fully-exposed branch. Its call is a soft 'check', repeated two or three times, and a sharper 'tick, tick-tick'; when it is more agitated it utters a harsh 'chack' and a 'trrt', almost like the note of the sedge warbler. Does not depend on fenland vegetation for food, and is found in bushy areas with thick undergrowth, neglected gardens and woodland margins.

Marsh warbler *Acrocephalus palustris* 12.5 cm

Very hard to distinguish from Blyth's reed warbler and – in most cases – from the reed warbler, especially young birds in autumn, when the rump is brown-beige. In spring, the marsh warbler is often pale, its upper parts a greenish-grey fawn and the whole of its underparts are an even, whitish, fawn-tinged lemon yellow. The legs are pale. The very lively song is full of imitative sounds; performed full-blast it is fluent, full of trills and mimicry, but the tempo can also be more restrained. Interwoven nasal, repetitive 'tzeh-bii' and fast, whirring sequences are typical. Both sexes sing. The call is a short harsh 'check'. The marsh warbler prefers dense lush vegetation like nettles, and is commonly found beside ditches and half-overgrown ponds, less often near larger lakes where reed warblers also occur. Rare in Britain and Ireland.

Reed warbler *Acrocephalus scirpaceus* 12.5 cm

The *Acrocephalus* warblers on this page are more or less indistinguishable in the field except for their song. Many reed warblers, however, have deeper and darker-coloured upper parts, darker breasts and legs and flatter foreheads/crowns than marsh warblers – they look angrier. The reed warbler lacks the eye-stripes and heavily-streaked plumage of the sedge warbler. The song, rather monotonous and laboured, is a flow of short notes, grating and repetitive, interwoven with imitations of other birds. The performance is like the sedge warbler's, but slower and lacking the changes of tempo and bright-voiced trills. The call is a low 'cherr'. The suspended nest is skilfully built in *Phragmites*.

Blyth's reed warbler

Marsh warbler

Reed warbler

Blyth's reed warbler

juvenile   autumn

Marsh warbler

autumn
juvenile

Reed warbler

Great reed warbler *Acrocephalus arundinaceus* 19 cm

The size of a small song thrush. Unlike the reed warbler it looks a heavyweight when clambering around in the reeds; the dead ones rustle and the live ones bend under its weight. In flight, the pale fawn rump stands out in contrast to the other upper parts. Its extraordinary song is incredibly noisy and coarse in tone. In form it resembles the reed warbler's, consisting of themes enunciated one to three times each, including harsh croaks and high falsetto howls and squeaks. The phrases are short and well spaced, and most often begin with two harsh croaks starting with a 'k', e.g. 'krr-krr, tsiep, kerretsiepp, tsiee, tsiee, kerre-kerre, krik-krik-krik, tchi-tchi . . .'. Frequents *Phragmites* beds beside many types of fresh water and lives on insects and small fish, turning to berries during the autumn. Rare in Britain and Ireland.

Sedge warbler *Acrocephalus schoenobaenus* 13 cm

Easy to distinguish in the field except from the (rare) aquatic warbler. In summer the upper parts are often fairly pale; the white eye-stripe combined with a dark stripe through the eye, dark crown, broad pale fringes to the wing feathers and rust-coloured rump are the most striking characteristics. Young birds often have a distinct brownish-fawn crown and faint blotches on the breast in autumn. The hoarse and croaking parts of the sedge warbler's song resemble that of the reed warbler, but the tempo is more hectic and there are long trills, often preceded by an accelerating creaking 'trr'. The bird often makes a short flappy song flight while the performance is in full swing. Its calls are a harsh 'chack' and a bright creaky 'trrr'. Insects and their larvae are its main diet.

Aquatic warbler *Acrocephalus paludicola* 12.5 cm

The distinct and invariably more conspicuous head and back stripes and striated flanks distinguish it from the sedge warbler. Young birds are a striking straw yellow in autumn. Its skulking habits are reminiscent of a grasshopper warbler, but its song resembles the sedge warbler's, although more restrained, with shorter phrases. Its call, too, resembles the sedge warbler's. Rare in western Europe, but occasionally seen in wetland vegetation or reed-beds. Wintering areas and migration routes are virtually unknown.

Great reed warbler

Sedge warbler

Aquatic warbler

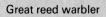

Great reed warbler

Sedge warbler

juvenile
autumn

juvenile
autumn

Aquatic warbler

Whinchat

Stonechat

Whinchat *Saxicola rubetra* 12.5 cm

Often perches in the tops of bushes, thistles, or on barbed wire, but is easily over-looked because its motley colours blend so perfectly with the surroundings. The broad pale eye-stripe, pale chin, speckled back and the short tail, frequently flicked, distinguish it from the stonechat, as well as the conspicuous white tail markings displayed in flight, especially in spring. All whinchats are speckled in autumn, but with varying colours from greyish fawn to deep red ochre. Because the song is extremely variable, often incoherent and capricious, it can easily pass unnoticed. The basic element is a fast crackly twittering, often including some mimicry. The alarm call is a persistent 'ju teck-teck'. Open rough grassland, especially with ditches, drier fenland, moors and heaths are favoured breeding areas. It lives on various insects and their larvae and spiders and snails taken from the ground or from flowers.

Stonechat *Saxicola torquata* 12.5 cm

Both sexes are distinguished from the whinchat in spring by a dark throat (some-times greyish fawn in females), the absence of an eye-stripe, and the longer, com-pletely dark tail. In autumn, however, young birds may have pale throats, but never prominent eye-stripes or well-defined back markings. The upper parts of the male vary from brown to black. The song is a hasty scratching twitter similar to the whitethroat's, sometimes produced during the dancing song flight. When annoyed or alarmed it emits a 'vit track-track', the latter part being rather hollow like the sound of two stones being knocked together (hence the name). Stonechats occur in open areas, usually dry and sandy ones and often breed on heathland and also, in western Europe, on coastal slopes. The diet is the same as the whinchat's, but nearly all food is caught on the ground. It often perches on stones, unlike the whinchat, as well as the tops of plants.

Whinchat

Stonechat

♀

Whinchat

♂ autumn

♂

♀ juvenile
autumn

♂

♀

Stonechat

Wheatear   Bluethroat

Wheatear   *Oenanthe oenanthe*   15 cm

Unmistakable. Around the Mediterranean and in Asia, however, a number of species have very similar tail markings. Appearances vary greatly in autumn, making the sex and age of individual birds difficult to determine, but birds with a white eye-stripe, black patch through the eye, grey with spotted brown upper parts and orange-cream underparts are adult males. Year-old males in spring have brown, not black, wings. Juveniles moult into their autumn plumage in July and August. The song is a continuous, ragged, gravelly ditty which begins with a few calls – harsh but slightly grasping 'weet' sounds which are sometimes also woven into the song. This is usually produced in a song flight. The alarm call is 'shack'. Breeds in open country with stony patches, on moorland and near the coast.

Bluethroat   *Luscinia svecica*   14 cm

Sparsely found (mostly in northeastern Europe) in swampy areas, osier beds and on lake shores. *Cyanecula*, the southern race, has a white throat patch while *svecica*, which breeds in northern Scandinavia, has a red one. Scandinavian birds appear regularly in western Europe during migrations in May and August–September, in waterlogged and scrubby vegetation. The throat markings of autumn birds and of females during spring are sometimes a deep ochre but they vary a great deal. This unobtrusive bird spends most of its time skulking on the ground, often flicking its tail. It tends to hide the splendour of its breast, so that the tail markings are often the main means of identification. The full song is an endless effervescence of bright delicate notes, rapidly trilling and frequently with accelerating bell notes 'tritritritritri ...' or 'tingtingtingting ...'. The call is also woven in – a harsh but rather thin 'tchak', often uttered as 'tsi tchak-tchak'. The diet is insects and, occasionally, berries and fruit.

Wheatear

Bluethroat

Wheatear

juvenile

♂

♀

juvenile

♀

autumn

Wheatear

juvenile

♂ autumn

♂
white-spotted

Bluethroat ♀

juvenile

autumn

♂

Bearded reedling ♀ juvenile

Bearded reedling   *Panurus biarmicus*   16.5 cm

An easy-to-spot bird. Adult females sometimes have a dark eye-patch and, in rare cases, a varying amount of dark crown marking. It is common for females to have dark striations on their backs. Juveniles moult into adult dress in July–September. Often revealed by its characteristic 'tying' and 'ping' calls, rapidly and nervously repeated, sometimes followed by a protracted rolling 'tyirr'. The subdued song is a trisyllabic creak. The flight on whirring wings, usually a low skimming above the reeds, is slow and uncertain. In autumn, when *Phragmites* beds are sometimes overpopulated, bearded reedlings often form a flock high above the reeds before making an unusually firm and rapid migratory beeline for another lake, possibly many kilometres away. There are three or four broods every year, and young birds hatched early can reproduce within the year. The population fluctuates drastically, depending on the severity of the winter. Lives on insects, spiders and, for most of the year, *Phragmites* seeds.

The bearded reedling, centre right, p. 121, is a juvenile ♂.

Penduline tit   *Remiz pendulinus*   11 cm

Like the bearded reedling, a rather unusual bird. Unafraid but rather aloof, it reminds one of a tit. The call is noticeable all the year round, mostly by the gentle gasping 'ziii' or 'ziiiy'. The subdued song consists of slow variations on the call. It builds a skilfully-constructed pouch-shaped nest secured to the outermost end of a branch hanging over the water. One of the principal building materials is the 'down' of bulrushes. Wetlands with bulrushes are its favoured habitat, especially if there are willow, poplar or tamarisk trees. It lives mostly on insects. Rare outside its breeding/wintering areas.

Bearded reedling

Penduline tit

Bearded reedling

♂

♂

♀

♂

Penduline tit

♂

juvenile

Yellowhammer   *Emberiza citrinella*   16.5 cm

Extremely variable plumage. Young females in their first winter often have all-over greyish-fawn and chestnut markings. The chestnut rump is characteristic in all plumages. Food is found by hopping on the ground, often in a crouched posture, but flocks often perch in bushes. Between February and July the male has a two-part characteristic song – high scraping notes followed by a long melancholy closing note 'tzi-tzi-tzi-tz-tzi-tzi-tzeeh'. The alarm call is a short 'tsick'. From its perch, often a bush-top or telephone wire, it makes a rasping 'dzee'. Usually found in farmland, scrub, coastal areas with gorse, even in wetland areas with bushes and open woodland. It feeds on various seeds and, during the nesting season, mainly on insects.

Cirl bunting   *Emberiza cirlus*   16.5 cm

The male is unmistakable. The female resembles the yellowhammer, but is more clearly streaked, buff rather than yellow beneath, has a pale stripe above and below the eye, and, most characteristic, a grey or olive brown rump. Autumn birds are variable, best identified by rump colour. The habits are the same as the yellow-hammer but it prefers the country – more trees, bushes, heaths, scrubs, gardens and woodland edges and it is often more difficult to encounter. In autumn and winter it can also be found on open farmland, feeding on seeds and insects. The song is a prolonged wooden rattling, like a lesser whitethroat. Its call is a drawn-out 'tsiip' in flight, sometimes a vibrant 'sisitsip'.

Ortolan bunting   *Emberiza hortulana*   16.5 cm

Easily identified by the pale, sulphur-yellow eye-ring. In spring the olive grey 'square' head, whitish yellow of the thick drooping moustache and pink bill are striking, together with the reddish-fawn underparts. The first half of the song has a beautiful timbre, rather like the great tit's, but the second half is more melancholy, descending in pitch. The song varies, but is much more tuneful than other buntings. The call is a short 'chip', although migrant birds use 'sie', often followed by a short 'tupp' in a characteristically regular alternating pattern. The ortolan favours open farmland with scattered trees and copses, heathland scrub and meadows, often close to wetlands. Lives on seeds and insects, particularly butterfly larvae, and migrates to tropical Africa in August–September, returning in May. Occasionally seen on migration in northwestern Europe.

Yellowhammer

Cirl bunting

Ortolan bunting

Yellowhammer ♀

Yellowhammer ♂

Cirl bunting ♀

Cirl bunting ♂

Ortolan bunting ♂

Ortolan bunting ♀

Corn bunting *Emberiza calandra* 18 cm

Recognized by its large size, lark-like plumage, absence of white on the tail and stout beak. Frequents open farmland and is often easy to find because it likes to perch on telephone wires and roadside fences. From his perch the male 'sings' a sequence which starts with a fast chirping and then turns into an extended glass-crunching or key-rattling sound. He flies to and from his song perch, and during the song, with fast, shallow wing beats and dangling legs. Corn buntings sometimes flock with yellowhammers outside the breeding season. The calls are a low but harsh 'tick', and a softly rolling 'dchrrut'. Lives on seeds and some insects.

Yellow-breasted bunting *Emberiza aureola* 15 cm

A handsome and easily spotted northeastern European bird. The female has yellow underparts, distinct head markings (the bar on her crown is often clearly visible) and white wing bars. Year-old males vary during spring and are sometimes identical to females. Juveniles on autumn migration have light straw-coloured underparts, broad eye-stripes and wing bars and heavily streaked rumps which are similar to females in autumn. The song varies, but is most reminiscent of the ortolan bunting, with tinges of the sedge warbler. The call is a short, sharp 'tsick' or 'tsi'. Breeding areas are lush, often waterlogged meadows, and fens and bogs with willows, birches or alders. Migration is to southeast Asia in August, returning in early June.

Reed bunting *Emberiza schoeniclus* (see picture p. 127) 14–16 cm

The summer male is unmistakable, but the female and all autumn birds have variable markings. However, their fawn and chestnut coloration, behaviour and shape distinguish them from all other buntings in the area. The rustic bunting (*E. rustica*) and the little bunting (*E. pusilla*), which breed in the taiga region, are very rarely seen in western Europe in a reed bunting habitat during their migration; notice the difference in the beak shape and in the cheek and breast markings. A common and widespread bird wherever there are wetlands. Their presence is often revealed by the delicately long-drawn-out call 'tsiiu', often uttered from the top of a clump of plants. The tail is often flicked, and the bird dives to the ground when danger approaches. The song varies, but is slow, raucous and chirruping with a whirring coda. The flight call is a low hoarse 'chup'. On migration and in winter, small flocks can even be seen in scrub, fields and gardens a long way from water.

Corn bunting

Yellow-breasted bunting

Reed bunting

124–125

Corn bunting

Yellow-breasted bunting

♂

first year
♂

♀

juvenile ♀ autumn

♂ autumn

Yellowhammer

Cirl bunting
juvenile
♀
autumn

Cirl bunting
♂ autumn

Ortolan bunting
juvenile
autumn

Yellow-breasted bunting ♀ juvenile   autumn

♂

Reed bunting

♂ autumn

♀ autumn

Little bunting

Rustic bunting
juvenile

autumn

autumn

Reed bunting

juvenile
♀ autumn

Ornithological & Conservation Societies in Britain and Ireland

Most countries and some major towns and cities have their own ornithological society: your library should be able to provide the address. Usually these societies hold regular indoor and field meetings – an ideal introduction to the area and the subject – and publish regular reports.

National bodies:

British Trust for Ornithology, Beech Grove, Tring, Herts.
(organize bird ringing, censuses and a wide variety of studies designed for cooperative participation by amateurs. *Bird Study* quarterly, *BTO News* every two months).

Irish Wildbird Conservancy, Royal Irish Academy, 19 Dawson Street, Dublin 2.
(fulfils a similar role in Ireland to the B.T.O.).

Royal Society for the Protection of Birds, The Lodge, Sandy, Beds.
(reserve network available to members, junior branch Young Ornithologists' Club organizes cooperative fieldwork. Colour magazine *Birds* quarterly).

Wildfowl Trust, Slimbridge, Gloucestershire.
(network of wildfowl reserves and collections available, organize winter wildfowl counts. Regular bulletin, *Wildfowl News*, and *Wildfowl*, published annually).

Further Reading

The following selection of books is suggested for you to follow up your interest in birds and their lives. Some deal with identification, some with fieldwork and equipment, and some with biology and ecology. All will prove useful sources of further titles.

Batten, L., Flegg, J., Sorenson, J., Wareing, M., Watson, D. and Wright, D., *Birdwatchers' Year*, T. & A. D. Poyser, 1973.
Brown, L., *The British Birds of Prey*, Collins, 1976.

Brunn, B. and Singer, A., *The Hamlyn Guide to the Birds of Britain and Europe*, Hamlyn, 1974.

Campbell, B. and Ferguson-Lees, J., *A Field Guide to Birds' Nests*, Constable, 1972.

Cramp, S., Bourne, W. R. P. and Saunders, D., *The Seabirds of Britain and Ireland*, Collins, 1974.

Durman, R. (ed.), *Bird Observatories in Britain and Ireland*, T. & A. D. Poyser, 1976.

Ennion, E. A. R., *The Lapwing*, Methuen, 1949.

Fisher, J. and Flegg, J., *Watching Birds*, T. & A. D. Poyser, 1974; Penguin Books, 1978 (in paperback).

Flegg, J., *Discovering Bird Watching*, Shire Publications, 1973.

Flegg, J. J. M., *Binoculars, Cameras and Telescopes*, B. T. O. Field Guide, 1971.

Fry, C. H. and Flegg, J. J. M., *World Atlas of Birds*, Mitchell Beazley, 1974.

Gooders, J., *Where to Watch Birds*, Deutsch, 1967; Pan Books, 1977 (in paperback).

Gooders, J., *Where to Watch Birds in Europe*, Deutsch, 1970; Pan Books, 1977 (in paperback).

Hayman, P. and Burton, P., *The Birdlife of Britain*, Mitchell Beazley, 1976.

Heinzel, H., Fitter, R. and Parslow, J., *The Birds of Britain and Europe*, Collins, 1972.

Hollom, P. A. D., *The Popular Handbook of British Birds*, H. F. & G. Witherby, 1971.

Hollom, P. A. D., *The Popular Handbook of Rarer British Birds*, H. F. & G. Witherby, 1970.

Lack, D., *Ecological Adaptations for Breeding in Birds*, Methuen, 1968.

Lack, D., *Population Studies of Birds*, Oxford University Press, 1966.

Mead, C. J., *Bird Ringing*, B. T. O. Field Guide, 1974.

Moreau, R. E., *The Palearctic-African Bird Migration System*, Academic Press, 1972.

Ogilvie, M. A., *Ducks of Britain and Europe*, T. & A. D. Poyser, 1975.

Porter, R. F., Willis, I., Christensen, S. and Nielsen, B. P., *Flight Identification of European Raptors*, T. & A. D. Poyser, 1974.

Sharrock, J. T. R. (ed.), *The Atlas of Breeding Birds in Britain and Ireland*, B. T. O., 1977.

Thomson, A. L., *A New Dictionary of Birds*, Nelson, 1964.

Voous, K. H., *Atlas of European Birds*, Nelson, 1960.

Welty, J. C., *The Life of Birds*, Saunders, 1975.

Witherby, H. F., Jourdain, F. C. R., Ticehurst, N. F. and Tucker, B., *The Handbook of British Birds*, 5 vols, H. F. & G. Witherby, 1938–41.

Index

131